LEAPS OF FAITH

John !
You are a great
friend and inspiration.

[signature]

July 2020

LEAPS *OF* FAITH

AN IMMIGRANT'S ODYSSEY
OF STRUGGLE, SUCCESS, AND
SERVICE TO HIS COUNTRY

AMBASSADOR
M. OSMAN SIDDIQUE

Leaps of Faith
An Immigrant's Odyssey of Struggle, Success, and Service to his Country

F I R S T   E D I T I O N

Hardcover ISBN: 978-1-7344796-0-7
Paperback ISBN: 978-1-7344796-1-4
eBook ISBN: 978-1-7344796-2-1

Library of Congress Control Number: 2020900150

TP

TransconPublishing

To:
My wife, the love of my life;
My children, the joys of my life;
My parents, who gave me life.

CONTENTS

FOREWORD

I first met Osman Siddique in March of 1996 at a small dinner party at the Hay-Adams Hotel in Washington. The Oklahoma City bombing had happened about a year earlier and that night at the Hay-Adams, Osman thanked me for the statement I made right after the bombing urging that we, as a nation, not jump to conclusions about who was responsible. Many were certain the act had to have been carried out by Middle Eastern terrorists, and many American Muslims, good citizens like Osman, felt they too were under a cloud of suspicion. Then we soon learned the bomber was not a Muslim, but a deeply disturbed homegrown terrorist.

As I began my second term, in keeping with my commitment to have an administration that reflected the many faces of America, I appointed Osman Siddique as a U.S. Ambassador to Fiji, Nauru, Tonga, and Tuvalu, making him the first Muslim-American ambassador to serve as a chief of mission anywhere.

I had gotten to know Osman during the campaign season and I knew he was well qualified for the job. That decision was tested when Fiji became engulfed in turmoil that resulted in a coup. Osman handled the largely race-related crisis with deft and diplomacy. Ambassador Siddique's leadership demonstrated to the Fijian people what America stood for.

A few months later, I was happy to have Osman accompany me on my state visit to India and Bangladesh. It was gratifying to see him representing America and my administration on a visit to his motherland. After the trip, Osman served out the rest of his mission with dedication, skill, and integrity.

It's refreshing in this age of divisiveness to read the words of a man with an open mind and a good heart. But what shines forth the brightest in this memoir is Osman's unwavering faith—in himself, in his community, and, most assuredly, in his country. Hillary and I join in thanking Osman and his wife Catherine for their friendship and service, and we send our best to their wonderful children—Omar, Julene, Leila, and Zachary. We have appreciated our time getting to know the Siddique family, as I am sure you'll appreciate getting to know them in the course of this delightful book.

Bill Clinton
APRIL 2020

CHAPTER ONE

Happy Birthday

U.S. Marine Colonel Cletus Davis, my defense attaché, burst into the room. He was slightly out of breath and I could tell he'd run up the stairs from his second-story office.

"Ambassador," he said, clicking his heels together in military fashion, "we have a situation."

"What is it?"

"We just received a report that there's been a paramilitary coup of some sort. The militia have taken over the parliament. The Prime Minister and his entire cabinet were there. Our understanding at this point is that several of them may have been summarily executed."

I tried to make sense of this news. The executions turned out to be false rumors, but that was the best information we had at the time. Executions or no executions, the government was being overthrown. There had been some rumblings of dissatisfaction, and I had reported on some disturbing signs of potential instability, but we had no actionable intelligence that anything of this scale had been brewing at this particular time.

I'd been ambassador for less than a year and I was becoming well-adjusted to my new environment. First off, it was Fiji, a beautiful island country in the South Pacific. When the opportunity first presented itself, I imagined a job that entailed holding the American flag in one hand and a piña colada in the other. Initially, I'd had some trouble convincing our four children to uproot themselves and move 8,000 miles away from home. There were a few adjustments we had to make to our lifestyles once we got there, but everybody was on board now. We liked Fiji. We liked the sun and the water and the friendly Fijian people.

My ambassadorial responsibilities also included the small nations of Tonga, Tuvalu, and Nauru—all South Pacific island nations. Additionally, the consular district included Tahiti and other French Polynesian islands. These were not independent countries and so there were no full-fledged embassies, but they still came under our scope of consular responsibility. And it was always fun to brag about this fun fact: my consular district was the largest in the U.S. State Department. Of course, ninety-eight percent of it was water and so the bragging was always done tongue-in-cheek.

I also liked the post because it gave me a chance to bring something to these countries that perhaps a lot of ambassadors could not, and that was my business know-how. Before I'd divested my business interests to take the position, I'd been running the travel management company that I had started back in 1976, our nation's bicentennial year. It had grown into one of the largest and most successful in the country. I had also co-founded a worldwide consortium of independent travel management companies that had grown into a mega enterprise. In 1992, I had been greatly flattered by a two-page spread in *Forbes* magazine entitled "In the Shadow of American Express." I knew I had something I could offer these small countries. We could work with them to bring investment dollars and improve their economies.

Now my ambassadorship was going to be tested in no uncertain terms. Ironically, the day had started out as an especially good one. For one thing, it was my birthday. My fiftieth. I was now half a century old. I wasn't supposed to know about it, but I suspected a surprise party was in store for me that evening. No doubt my wife was back at our house organizing a delicious Italian meal for a gathering of friends and embassy co-workers. Just like Catherine. She came from an Italian family and, boy, did she know how to prepare Italian food. Of course, Italian cuisine wasn't anything I'd been very familiar with growing up in Bangladesh. I'd learned to like it after I'd moved to the States, and when Catherine came along, I liked it even more.

That morning, she had practically shooed me out of the house. "You're going to be late," she'd insisted, even though I was right on time. I let her shoo me away, presuming she had a lot of dinner preparation to take care of and other party details to wrap up. My plan was to come home that evening, open the door, and look as astonished as I could possibly look when everybody jumped out and yelled "Surprise!"

And that would not have been the only pleasant surprise of the day. Before Davis's jarring arrival into my office, my Deputy Chief of Mission Ron McMullen had come into my office holding an envelope. "This just came for you," he'd said. "It's got the presidential seal."

It did indeed. The heavy-stock envelope was trimmed in red, white, and blue. The return address read simply: "The White House."

"Read it out loud," someone suggested. My whole staff was in my office. Minutes earlier, Phyllis Williams, my personal assistant had walked into the room with a cake, everybody trailing her and singing "Happy Birthday."

I took the envelope from my DCM and carefully opened it. I slipped the letter out of it and began to read it to the group.

> *Dear Osman;*
>
> *Happy 50th Birthday! Hillary and I send our very best wishes for health and happiness in the coming year.*
>
> *Sincerely,*
> *Bill Clinton*

Of course he'd address it "Osman" and not "Ambassador Siddique," and of course, he'd sign it "Bill Clinton" and not "President Clinton." Just like him. What a great honor to receive a personal birthday greeting from the president of the United States. I smiled to the staff. Inside, I was positively beaming. I'd liked President Clinton from the moment we'd met. He had a way of speaking directly to you, and listening intently to you, to where you felt like there was nobody else in the room, even if it was a crowded one. Somehow, he managed to remember me. When the Fiji ambassadorship had come open, the president had chosen me for the position, our nation's very first Muslim ambassador.

Reading the letter, I reveled in the moment. But the moment was short-lived.

Moments afterward, something caught my eye out of my top-story embassy window. It wasn't anything tangible. It's just that the street below had suddenly become eerily empty. A dark cloud had formed in the sky and it cast an ominous shadow over what had been a beautiful sunny day, adding to the eeriness. Within minutes, I noticed people beginning to enter the street. There was some kind of commotion going on. Then the lights in the embassy began to flicker. Soon they went out. The computers went dark. The embassy generators kicked on and power was shortly restored but I wondered what was happening.

Seconds later, my defense attaché burst in and I had my answer.

Back outside my window, I could see that the small crowd had become larger and had slowly turned itself into a mob. Looking closer, I could see people armed with machetes and sticks. Rocks and stones were being thrown through windows. I noticed smoke coming from stores and government buildings. Quickly, we discovered that telephone service had been cut.

My mind raced. I needed to take action. I knew things would be happening very quickly. I also needed to make sure my family was all right. Our house was two blocks away from the parliament building. I'd had ambassadorial training. I'd learned to fire multiple weapons, even how to drive a car evasively. I'd been briefed on crisis situations, but I hadn't expected this. This was Fiji—a tropical island paradise! So much for the piña coladas.

After his stunning announcement, my defense attaché had nothing further to add. Clicking his heels together once again, he turned to go. Then he paused a moment. "Happy birthday, Mr. Ambassador," he said, then he slipped out of the room.

CHAPTER TWO

Birth of a Nation

I WASN'T THE FIRST AMBASSADOR in the family. My father was ambassador to Tanzania and several other East African countries. But he wasn't a U.S. ambassador. He was an ambassador from Pakistan. His title, however, was High Commissioner, which is how members of the British Commonwealth, like Pakistan, refer to those whom we call ambassadors.

This was before 1971, back when our little portion of the world was known as East Pakistan. In March of 1971, the independence movement would be born for the creation of Bangladesh. "East Pakistan" would belong to Pakistan no longer. The movement precipitated a liberation war and Bangladesh genocide at the hands of the Pakistani army. By December of that year, the new nation of Bangladesh would be recognized internationally.

In fact, my father's nationality went back further than East Pakistan. When my father, M. Osman Ghani (in the Muslim and Arab world you don't necessarily adopt your father's last name), was born in 1912, the country was known as East Bengal and was part of the British Empire along with India. In 1947, three years before my birth, Pakistan became free of British rule while remaining a member of the British Commonwealth (known today as the Commonwealth of Nations), a group of free and equal states composed mostly of former colonies of the Empire. At this time, East Bengal became East Pakistan and was fashioned into a province of Pakistan even though it was over a thousand miles distant. In retrospect, it seems inevitable that there would ultimately be an independence movement for East Pakistan.

But my father's interest was not necessarily in the politics of the region. My father was a man of education. As a boy, he was an extraordinary student. His father, my grandfather, a respected village elder, was a resourceful farmer. It was expected that my father, the first-born son, would follow in his footsteps, leaving school as soon as he was old enough to work in the fields. But many of my father's teachers saw brilliance in him and went to my grandfather and pleaded with him not to take him out of school. He reluctantly acceded. My father stayed in school, ultimately leaving the small village to attend college where he did exceedingly well. He then acquired his masters from Dhaka University where he attracted sufficient attention from his teachers that he was awarded the esteemed Lytton Overseas Scholarship. The scholarship was given annually by the British Empire to two students of merit: one a Hindu Indian and one a Muslim Indian. My father qualified for the latter and was sent to London University. Nothing at that time could have been more prestigious than traveling to England to study.

My father had never been so far from home. He first had to take a train twelve-hundred miles from Calcutta to Mumbai. Then he boarded a boat for a twenty-eight-day journey that took him through the Indian Ocean, up the Red Sea, through the Suez Canal, across the Mediterranean, through the Strait of Gibraltar, out into the North Atlantic, and up to Liverpool, before another train ride to London. He told us of nerves and sleeplessness and rough seas. Once in England, he was beset with homesickness, but nevertheless excelled in his studies. He stayed in a small boarding house with a few other students with whom he made friends, but he missed Bengali cuisine. Fortunately, he found an Indian restaurant on Regent Street called Veeraswamy, which is there to this day. He and his friends would save their money and once a month they would eat to their heart's content at Veeraswamy. My father returned home before the start of the Second World War with a PhD in chemistry and a remarkably bright future.

Settling in Dhaka, he became a professor at Dhaka University. By the time I came along, he was a professor, dean, and provost. Ultimately, he'd become vice chancellor, the equivalent in the British educational system to an American university president. My father worked frequently with American universities, setting up Dhaka University's first business school in collaboration with Indiana University and even receiving an honorary Doctorate of Science from the University of Colorado. American education was heavily valued by my father and that would extend to his children.

It has been nearly 100 years since that day my grandfather agreed to allow his first-born son to pursue education instead of farming. In all that time, nobody from the village has achieved more.

It would be after my father's retirement, in the late 1960s, that the government of Pakistan would call upon my father and appoint him to his ambassadorship. Who could have conceived then that some thirty years later, his son would also become an ambassador, representing the world's greatest economic and military power?

As far as my father's academic career path, what it meant for his four sons and five daughters was that education was paramount. We could not help but become educated. In time, my family would boast five PhDs, three vice chancellors, and one education minister. My nephew Kamal would be the founder of the Asian University for Women, established in Chittagong, Bangladesh in 2008, a university that admits women from all over the region solely on the basis of merit, nearly all of them on full scholarships.

My father made sure we all attended the best schools and while I was growing up, the best schools around Dhaka were the Jesuit schools run by Americans. Above all else, my father wanted to make sure we had a firm grasp of the English language. I started at Holy Cross School, graduated to Trinity School, went to middle school at Saint Mary's, and then acquired my high school diploma at Saint Gregory's.

Those are interesting names of schools for a Muslim kid to attend. I learned more than English; I learned the basics of other monotheistic religions. This was fine with my parents. My mother and father were both broad-minded and encouraged broad-mindedness in us, a trait that has served me well. "We are all people of the Book," my father used to say, meaning that we all—Jews, Christians, Muslims—have our roots in the same Abrahamic traditions. We were loyal to Islam and learned our religion well through home-tutoring, but we also had catechism classes at school.

I also learned discipline and decorum at those Jesuit schools. The teachers were strict. We had to show them respect, and we had to show our fellow students respect, as well. Discipline came at home, too, but mostly from our mother, Shamsun Nahar. Our father was busy with his career, but our mother was a simple homemaker. She wasn't educated like our father, but she was very smart. She'd administer appropriate punishment to us when we'd cross the line, but she showered us with love, too. With nine children, it was more or less organized chaos for my mother, but we felt loved, we felt safe, we felt secure.

Our lives were admittedly different than other East Pakistani families. We weren't very wealthy, but my father made a good honest living. He owned a car, which would have been a luxury for most families. It was a Chrysler Plymouth sedan, one of just three such cars in the city at the time. And so we lived comfortably. But the main advantage for us children was the education and the exposure to the outside world that the education gave us.

Music was also important in our family, but this was true in most Bengali households. The Bengali culture is steeped in music and dance, as well as literature and art and theater. Rabindranath Tagore won the Nobel Prize in literature in 1913 for his sensitive and refined Bengali poetry. The rich traditions of Bengali culture were instilled in us early. All of us kids played some kind of musical instrument. My youngest sister, Florin, learned the sitar and my eldest brother, Farruk, boasted the first Fender Hawaiian electric guitar in the country. I played the accordion and piano, though I had no formal training, and fantasized about becoming a famous crooner. This love and appreciation for music continues in our family to this day. My daughter Julene acquired her master's in composition from the Royal College of Music in London, the same school that has graduated the likes of Gustav Holst, Neville Marriner, and Andrew Lloyd Webber. She also acquired a master's in music and development from the School of Oriental and African Studies at the University of London. Julene is now a rising composer, with her works frequently performed live in Bahrain and Bulgaria, at last allowing me to vicariously live, through her, my musical aspirations.

I did fair in school, but nobody was likely to confuse me with my father when it came to academic success. I got by. But a career in academia wasn't anything I was necessarily seeking anyway. It's hard to say what I was seeking at a young age. I knew one thing: I was intrigued by America. I'd been exposed to much of American culture through movies and books, and the lifestyle looked good to me. I saw the Elvis Presley movie *Blue Hawaii* and America seemed filled with fun and beautiful people. But I was not naïve. I saw other American movies, films like *Guess Who's Coming to Dinner* and *To Kill a Mockingbird*, films about racism and injustice. I knew America was not a perfect land. Nevertheless, it spoke to me of promise and opportunity.

But first, it was off to university. Like my father and older siblings before me, I enrolled at Dhaka University. This was the time that my father was serving as ambassador to Tanzania. But his ambassadorship was far from simple. This was when East Pakistan was heading down the road toward independence as Bangladesh. Outwardly, my father had to maintain a façade

of support for his office. Inwardly, he supported his people—
Bengalis. Years later, my father's Indian counterpart in Tanzania
in those days, Jagat S. Mehta, later to become India's foreign secretary, would write of my father's predicament in his book *The
Tryst Betrayed*.[1] "While he was officially obliged to represent
Pakistan, [my father's] sympathy was with the freedom movement led by Sheikh Mujibur Rahman." Mehta wrote of my father
and mother coming to see him and his wife "in the middle of
the night" to discuss ways in which to surreptitiously support
Sheikh Mujib while appearing faithful to Pakistan. As Mehta
put it, supporting Sheikh Mujib meant "near-fatal danger" for
our family. While I was at Dhaka University, so were my broth-
ers-in-law with their families. They were both senior professors
and married to my two eldest sisters, Nahar and Helen. The
university was a hotbed of the independence movement and
we were targets, along with other students and academics. The
danger was real, as we knew firsthand. My mother had a cousin
whose husband, Sadat Ali, was an American-educated professor
at Dhaka University. One night he was abducted and was never
seen again. My eldest brother, who was a professor at another
university, was forced into hiding, finding refuge for himself and
his family in our ancestral village. Our lives were in jeopardy.
And my father was being watched. My father's first secretary, as
Mehta writes, "had been told to keep a vigilant eye on his 'boss.'"
My father had to think of us.

It was a terrible conundrum he found himself in, but he
handled it with honor and diplomatic skill. In meetings with

---

[1]   *The Tryst Betrayed: Reflections on Diplomacy and Development*, Penguin,
2010.

Tanzanian president Julius Nyerere in the capital city of Dar es Salaam, he was reminded in no uncertain terms that Tanzania had close ties with China. China had close ties to Pakistan. Therefore, Tanzania would have no sympathy for the independence movement. Tanzania desired a strong Pakistani presence, which my father, as ambassador, was expected to provide. When hostilities would break out between India and Pakistan in December of 1971, he lowered the Pakistani flag and, along with his family, departed Dar es Salaam for London with the help of Jagat Mehta and cut his ties with Pakistan.

For us, in early 1971 while my father was walking the diplomatic tightrope between his ambassador duties to Pakistan and his loyalty to the Bengalis, the dangers were omnipresent. In March of that year, the Pakistani army launched a military assault on East Pakistan that would continue for months. Thousands of Bengali students, intellectuals, and politicians were ultimately massacred, many of them on the campus of Dhaka University.

Everything started on the night of March 25. The army encircled the university. They came with tanks, rocket launchers, automatic rifles, and machine guns. They initially sought out professors that had been instrumental in the liberation movement, quickly killing around a dozen of them. Then they attacked the student hall that housed the Independent Bangladesh Students Movement Council, massacring some 200 students. They entered other dormitories, indiscriminately killing students. They started a fire at a girls' dorm and then mowed down students trying to escape. They killed university staff members whether they were part of the movement or not.

From my apartment window, I saw some of the killings. At one point, I saw a group of students running and then falling in a hail of gunfire, the grisly scene lit up by flares the army troops would shoot high into the night sky. I imagined it was just a matter of time before the troops would enter the apartment I was in. Where would I hide? It seemed certain to me that I would not survive that night. By divine providence, my apartment was left alone and I escaped the campus two days later. March 25, 1971 became known as Black Night.

I had more or less been apolitical as a student. I imagine most of us students were. We were college kids, studying hard but having fun, too, and enjoying our newfound freedoms from home. But no one left standing after Black Night could remain neutral. We were Bengalis. We were not Pakistanis. Though we shared a religion, we did not share a culture or history. We were suppressed by a foreign power and now we were being annihilated. Black Night introduced me to the larger arena of geopolitical struggle. The world could be a very dangerous place. I survived that night, but something in me changed. My childhood innocence was lost.

In the months that followed, the international community would begin to take notice of what was happening in our corner of the world. What started out as a massacre quickly grew into genocide. It was a brutal, tragic start to a nation, but as my childhood ended, Bangladesh was born.

CHAPTER THREE

The Great Midwest

I DID NOT RETURN TO Dhaka University. The Bangladesh War for Liberation lasted nine months. The Pakistani military, along with Islamist militias, slaughtered what independent researchers believe was up to half a million Bengalis, although Bengali sources will often put that number closer to three million. Additionally, an indeterminate number of Bengali women and girls were raped and left pregnant after a fatwa in Pakistan declared that they could be taken as "booty of war." The Pakistani ruling clique and military junta were unworthy of the good people of Pakistan, committing atrocities that left a tragic and indelible dark spot on the collective memory of the nation. An estimated eight million people fled Bangladesh during the war and another thirty million became displaced from their homes.

I left, too. Bangladesh was in turmoil and America was calling. My father's earlier collaboration with Indiana University provided a link for me to continue my studies in the United States and I was accepted as a special student there. In the summer of 1972, I left London, where I'd been staying, for New York City. I would stay a couple of weeks in New York before flying on to Indiana. Meeting me at JFK airport was Dr. Rashiduzzaman, a visiting senior fellow at Columbia University. Dr. Rashiduzzaman was a former teacher of mine at Dhaka University and a close family friend. He drove me from the airport to his apartment close to Columbia, but nevertheless in a Harlem neighborhood. It was the middle of the night and I wouldn't get a good look at my surroundings until the next day. These were not good times for Harlem. This was years before the area's resurgence and my stay would open my eyes to the realities of America. In the light of the morning, I saw decayed buildings and poverty. The ragged people passing by on the street outside wore faces of despair. This was certainly not the hopeful America I saw in *Blue Hawaii* and I was quite taken aback. There was crime, too, of course. Once during my time there, Dr. Rashiduzzaman hosted a dinner party. One of the guests failed to show but called later that evening from the hospital. He'd been mugged going into Dr. Rashiduzzaman's building.

Dr. Rashiduzzaman and his wife forbade me from venturing out at night, but were gracious and kind hosts and were happy to accompany me around the city during the daytime so that I could see New York. Many parts of Manhattan stood in stark contrast to what I saw in Harlem. I loved the buzz of Times Square and Fifth Avenue. I was awed by the sight of hundreds of yellow cabs snaking through the streets, big old American cars that were seemingly everywhere. From Battery Park, I could see the Statue of Liberty and I got goosebumps and felt my eyes moisten at the sight.

In August, I boarded a TWA plane at LaGuardia for Indianapolis. From there, it was onto a Trailways bus for the hour-long trip to a place called Bloomington. It was hot that particular August in Indiana. My father, with his English training, wanted me to arrive as a gentleman. He insisted that I pack a suit, a decent overcoat, and an umbrella. I had nothing more than a small duffel bag and a briefcase and the only way I could see to carry my suit without getting it all wrinkled was to wear it. And so there I was getting off the bus into the steamy August air wearing my dark pinstripe suit, starched white shirt, and tie, with my overcoat slung over my arm, and holding both my briefcase and an umbrella. The only thing missing was a black fedora.

The Foreign Students Office, knowing of my arrival, had sent a young French student to meet me. I wandered a short time until I saw him, a kid wearing cutoff shorts, a t-shirt, and flip-flops holding a sign with my name on it. As I approached him, he gazed right past me, past the overdressed young gentlemen coming towards him, no doubt looking for a more appropriately attired traveler. Who, on a hot August day, would be expecting a student dressed in a pinstripe suit and tie complete with overcoat and umbrella?

"I'm him," I said, pointing to the French student's sign.

"Huh?" he replied.

"Osman Siddique. That's me."

"You're ... Siddique?"

"Yes, that's me. I'm the one you're waiting for."

The French student looked me up and down, saying nothing but appearing flummoxed. Finally, he motioned me to his car and shortly after, dropped me in all of my sartorial splendor at the Foreign Students Office. There, I met with the coordinator who had my admission papers and, after filling out some forms, I was taken to Foley Hall to my dorm room where I promptly changed clothes. My roommate was a graduate student in the library science program. David McGee was kind and welcoming and he took me around the dorm, showing me the cafeteria and laundry room and pointing out where something called a "restroom" was, which I quickly ascertained was not a place to rest. I had a good grasp of the English language, but obviously had some work ahead of me when it came to translating the countless idioms, expressions, and euphemisms.

My father's counterpart at Indiana was the highly revered Herman B Wells, a man who would ultimately tally some seventy years of service with the school and for whom the university library is now named. (The "B", he would tell me, stood for nothing and was therefore never followed by a period.) Indiana owes much of what it is today to Dr. Wells. He was chancellor when I was there and would remain so, at least in an honorary capacity, until the year 2000 when he would pass away at the age of ninety-seven. His office had left a note for me in the Foreign Students Office inviting me to see him. When I met Dr. Wells, I was struck by his graciousness and kindness. He asked about my parents, whom of course he knew. They'd kept in touch and remained good friends. My younger brother, Yousef, would eventually follow me to IU where he would get his MBA. Years later, Yousef would be instrumental in setting up a fellowship in the joint names of our father and Dr. Wells. The fellowship was established as a faculty exchange program between the business administration colleges of both Indiana University and Dhaka University, recognizing the vision of both of these educational stalwarts. (Yousef currently leads a very prominent consulting practice in the oil and energy sector.)

In his office, Dr. Wells asked, among other things, how I was getting along and inquired about my financial situation, wanting to know that I'd be able to make ends meet during my time there. I had some savings, I assured him, and was planning on finding a part-time job. Truthfully, I hadn't thought very far ahead. My plan was to take things semester by semester. A few weeks later, I received a letter from the dean's office. I'd been awarded a fellowship that would pay for fifty percent of my tuition. I knew it must have been arranged by Dr. Wells.

Not long after that, I received a note from the chancellor's office, an invitation to Dr. Wells's house for dinner. Dr. Wells was a single man and would remain so his entire life, but his mother was present for dinner. She was ninety years old but was alert and talkative and she liked to paint. Dinner was delightful but Dr. Wells had an even bigger surprise for me—a concert at the Musical Arts Center. The Indiana University School of Music, today called the Indiana University Jacobs School of Music, was, and remains, one of the top music schools in the world. The Musical Arts Center was the brainchild of Dr. Wells and had just opened that year. Dr. Wells had front row seats for us and, although my musical taste at the time was not necessarily inclined towards classical, I felt elated to be sitting next to the great Dr. Wells as his guest in the beautiful new Arts Center.

Dr. Wells was not the only member of the faculty who made me feel welcomed at Indiana, nor the only connection my father had. Dr. Lee C. Nehrt, professor of international business, had been a visiting professor at Dhaka University and knew my father. He, too, invited me to his home for dinner where his wife Ardith prepared a much-appreciated home-cooked meal. Afterward, Dr. Nehrt offered me a drink and played a classical record on a little phonograph. It was another delightful evening. Dr. Nehrt would become my advisor and mentor.

Since my undergraduate work had been interrupted, it took me a couple of semesters before I was admitted into Indiana's MBA program, with a major in marketing and a minor in international business. I had majored in economics at Dhaka, mainly because I didn't feel I was smart enough to pass the physics and science courses! I quickly learned that economics was no cakewalk, either, but it gave me a perspective on business that stuck with me and further stoked an interest I'd always had in marketing. I knew that sales and marketing were how businesses developed and nations grew. And America led the world in marketing. I was in the right place for it and I wanted a future in it.

I enjoyed my classes and I enjoyed the American system of academics. With the British system, you take a course, you write some papers, and at the end of the academic year, you take a final, which counts for about ninety percent of your grade. At Indiana, there were quizzes and mid-terms along the way and the final didn't count for as much. The professors were more accessible, too. At Dhaka, things were much more formal. You addressed your teacher "Sir," and you would never fraternize with him the way we sometimes did with our professors at Indiana. We respected our professors at Indiana, but we would also feel comfortable sitting down with them, maybe over coffee after class, for give-and-take discussions.

Of course, I missed home, but was buoyed by the friendliness of the students and faculty. I did surprisingly well socially at Indiana. I had long dark hair and grew a full mustache and the girls seemed to find me attractive in a sort of exotic way. I was certainly not the typical Midwestern American type they'd been used to. Female and male students alike seemed to take an interest in where I was from. Bangladesh was in the news and, by then, George Harrison had organized his "Concert for Bangladesh," a benefit show held in New York's Madison Square Garden featuring Bob Dylan, Eric Clapton, Ringo Starr, Billy Preston, and others. The concert and the subsequent album raised hundreds of thousands of dollars for relief for the refugees from the genocide.

In addition to "Concert for Bangladesh," the situation had garnered a lot of publicity from a trip Senator Ted Kennedy had made to the area to survey the refugee crisis firsthand. He came back with a scathing report entitled "Crisis in South Asia," which he presented to the U.S. Senate Judiciary Committee on Refugees. At the time, President Nixon had been backing Pakistan because of its alliance with China, a country Nixon was intent on establishing relations with. Because of the public outcry, stoked by George Harrison and by Ted Kennedy, each in dramatically different ways, Congress finally passed a bill banning arms sales to Pakistan. In 1972, Kennedy would travel back to Dhaka and receive a hero's welcome.

And so my fellow students had heard of my newly birthed homeland, but that didn't mean they were familiar with it. I got some strange questions from time to time. One student asked if we drank milk in Bangladesh and another asked if we had telephones. I took the questions in stride for they were always asked out of sincere curiosity.

The genuine kindliness towards a foreigner that I experienced was never more apparent than Thanksgiving break of my first semester. The Wednesday before Thanksgiving, the campus was shutting down and the dorms were emptying as students left to be with their families for the holiday. I had nowhere to go, of course. I wandered through the business building, stopping in front of a bulletin board to peruse the postings, maybe find some activity going on somewhere that weekend, however improbable that seemed. Around the corner, came a young man I remembered seeing in one of my classes.

Mike Winski introduced himself and then said, "What are you doing for Thanksgiving?"

I barely knew what Thanksgiving was. It hadn't occurred to me to do anything for it. "Sticking around here, I guess," I answered.

"But everything's going to be closed. The dorms, the dining halls, nothing will be open." Then he thought for a moment and said, "Wait here a second."

Mike went off and came back shortly, saying, "Hey, I just called my parents. You're coming home with me."

"I don't want to be any trouble," I said.

"Nonsense. My whole family's looking forward to meeting you."

I left to grab some things at my dorm and then Mike came by in his spanking new yellow Ford Mustang. It was a little over three hours to Mike's home in Michigan City, Indiana, a lot of the drive on highways, my first-ever highway ride in a car. About halfway there, it began to lightly snow. Mike had the radio on and, of all songs, "Summer Breeze" by Seals and Croft was playing as the flurries hit our windshield. Soon, Mike and I were both singing loudly along as the snow continued to fall. I felt warmed by the song and by the friendship of Mike who only hours before had been a complete stranger to me.

When we finally arrived at his sprawling, contemporary home, his parents welcomed me graciously and showed me to my own bedroom. Later, Mike's sisters and brother came in and the next day we all went to a relative's home where there must have been fifty family members sitting down to the biggest feast I had ever seen. Mike's was a Jewish family and their welcome of me to their dinner table as a Muslim was touching. Overall, it was an extraordinary introduction to an American holiday that I have loved ever since.

Back at school, while the fellowship award I'd received was helping to pay my tuition, I still found my savings quickly depleting for other expenses—room and board, books, and miscellaneous spending. One time, Elvis Presley came to play a concert at the assembly hall. Of course I'd seen Elvis in movies and had listened to his music back home. I was a fan. But the tickets were fifteen dollars and I did not have it. I wandered around the hall the night of the concert lamenting the fact that I could not get in to see such an American icon. To this day, it still bothers me that I did not beg, borrow, or steal to find a way into that concert. Years later, my children would find a recording of the concert online, turn it into a CD, and present it to me as a birthday gift.

To earn money, I knew I needed a job and I took part-time work in the dorm cafeteria and at the university library. The next fall, I would also clean up trash in the football stadium after the games for five dollars an hour. American football was unfamiliar to me and I attended few games as a fan. My sports growing up had been soccer and cricket. I went to several basketball games at Indiana, however. One could not help but do so. These were the beginning years of the Bobby Knight era and the basketball program was on the rise. In 1972-73, Coach Knight's team won the Big Ten Conference and made it to the Final Four of the NCAA Tournament. The Hoosiers would win the Big Ten every year I was there, ultimately winning the National Championship in 1976.

By my second year, I had saved enough money to buy a used car. In the paper, I spotted an ad for a 1966 Chevy Chevelle for $600. I called and spoke to the owner, a farmer's son who lived about an hour away. I told him I was interested and we agreed to meet out in front of a Bloomington restaurant that we both knew. At the agreed-upon time, I stood in front of the restaurant and watched as a young, heavyset man in a green Chevelle drove slowly up the street towards me. He looked at me, then looked ahead and drove past me. Shortly, he stopped and then backed up. Then he got out of the car and asked if I was the person interested in buying the car. I told him I was.

"I'll be honest," he said, "I wanted to keep driving. I wasn't expecting to see someone like you. You're not at all how you sounded on the phone. But then I thought, well, you look all right, anyway. So I'll sell you the car if you want it."

In all of my time in the great Midwest, it was the only incident of racism I experienced. It left me speechless. I wanted to ask what "someone like you" meant, but I let it go. Truthfully, I'm not sure I understood the implications at the time. I'd never experienced prejudice before and it wasn't until later that I actually processed the incident and fully realized the bigotry the young man was expressing. At least he was honest about it, I suppose. And he did sell me the car. Based on everything else I'd experienced, I took the incident as an aberration.

As my studies continued, I began thinking of my future. When I'd come to the States, I'd never really thought consciously of making it my permanent home. Now, the thought was crossing my mind. Nevertheless, my immediate focus remained on my education. I wanted more than just the MBA I'd been working towards. I wanted actual business experience and I wanted that experience to be with a Fortune 500 company. As graduation neared, recruiters began visiting the campus and I began to think about my life's next steps.

★ CHAPTER FOUR ★

Entrepreneur

As a soon-to-be MBA graduate, I had interest from half a dozen big companies including Continental Bank out of Chicago, and engine manufacturer Cummins out of Columbus, Indiana. But the company that really drew my attention was MetLife, a Fortune 500 company and one of the largest insurance and financial institutions in the United States. MetLife had just come out with its new, vaunted training program exclusively for MBAs. The program was designed to develop a cadre of professional executives. It was a fast-track program for building a pipeline of future leaders.

I liked the new program for several reasons, first and foremost because it encompassed cross-functional assignments in the core areas of its business including marketing and sales, finance, operations, and product development. I was going to learn about every facet of the business. Additionally, the program would allow me to partner with a mentor to receive coaching from a senior leader, participate in in-depth training work, develop strong networks with executives and program peers, and, finally, become part of the next generation of general managers. I liked the fact that MetLife recognized that to be a global company, it needed to develop future leaders who could work across geographic and business functions, and provide diversity in gender, ethnic, and racial backgrounds, as well as global experience.

My final interview was at MetLife's offices in Indianapolis and I could see that the recruiters appreciated my understanding of the position and my attitude towards it. They were telling me that most MBAs came to them with a chip on their shoulders expecting big salaries and top executive positions. Me, I was willing to put in the work.

MetLife hired me for a starting salary of $18,000, not bad for the mid-1970s. The only problem was that they wanted to put me in their Indianapolis office. Indianapolis was fine, but I'd set my sights on somewhere else. I had decided I wanted to live in Washington, D.C. For one thing, my brother Farruk, a Cornell University PhD in economics, lived there. He held a position with the World Bank. But more importantly, I came from a capital city and I had lived and traveled in other capital cities. And Washington, D.C. wasn't just any capital city; it was the core of the free world. All the news seemed to come out of Washington. Everything seemed to be happening there. These were the days of Watergate and I had watched the hearings and found myself intrigued by the political processes at work. Every branch of government was on display and I was captivated. Plus, it was a cosmopolitan city, with people from all over the world living and visiting there. I liked the energy of the city and it seemed the perfect place for me to be.

MetLife accepted my request and I made plans to move to D.C. First, however, came a ten-day training and orientation program at the MetLife headquarters, which were located at 1 Madison Avenue in New York City. The company flew me in and put me up at the Waldorf Astoria where they hosted all of the program attendees. It was all expenses paid and I enjoyed the luxury of the accommodations as well as the hotel's expensive culinary delights. This was certainly a different introduction to New York than my first one in Harlem! It was interesting to me that one of the participants in the orientation was the son of the president/CEO of Prudential Life. He didn't want anything handed to him, he told the rest of us. Life would have been easy at Prudential, but he wanted to prove his mettle in the business and felt that the only way to be really tested was at another company.

After orientation, it was on to D.C. where I was mentored by Ken Martin, the district sales manager at a suburban office. Ken was a young Southern gentleman, suave and always impeccably dressed. He taught me a great deal about interacting with people. "Before you can sell anything," he told me, "you've got to sell yourself. People have to know you and like you and come to trust you."

I observed how he trained and motivated sales executives as they made their cold calls. They'd uncover leads by calling lists of people on the phone for hours. It could be long, grueling, frustrating work. You faced rejection ninety-eight times out of

a hundred. Ken put his own spin on it. It was the law of proba-
bilities. Welcome the no's, he'd say. Every no gets you one step
closer to a yes. In time, I began thinking of it in another way. I
read where Babe Ruth struck out 1,330 times in his career, a
Major League record that stood for years. But nobody remem-
bers the strikeouts. Instead, the Babe was remembered for his
714 home runs.

I did well at MetLife. I learned a lot from Ken and I learned
a lot from the whole experience. There was talk of a promotion.
It would mean new responsibilities and a transfer to another
location. But after a year and a half, the true American dream
got a hold of me: I decided I'd like to own and operate my own
business. I'd been paying attention to the news and there was
a lot of talk about airline deregulation. The government had
control over airline routes and fares, with air transport essentially functioning like a utility. Airlines weren't subject to the
normal forces of supply and demand and their profits were
more or less guaranteed. The system had grown bureaucratic
and inefficient. Deregulation hearings were being held, led by
Senator Ted Kennedy. I remembered Kennedy, of course, from
his role in bringing the plight of Bangladesh to the attention of
the American public.

Deregulation appeared to be imminent. Free-market forces
would rule the skies and I saw an opportunity. I knew that
deregulation would mean a new plethora of fares and routes,
and even new airlines. That meant that travel and tourism companies would be an even more crucial component of the travel
experience. These, after all, were the days before Expedia and
Travelocity and Orbitz. I saw an opportunity to serve the corporate travel market, especially since I was located in such an

important hub as the Washington, D.C. market where thousands of businesspeople, diplomats, government officials, politicians, and lobbyists flew into and out of every day.

The big names in corporate travel back then were the likes of American Express, Thomas Cook, and Carlson Travel. I knew I could not compete with these giants right away. They had the large, IBM-type accounts all sewn up. But I saw an opening with smaller, mid-sized companies, a neglected group that I called orphan accounts. I could offer these smaller businesses something the big boys couldn't, especially with the level playing field that was opening up by way of deregulation, and the technology that was being spurred by it. I could provide hands-on personalized service that American Express and the others couldn't touch. In 1976, I took a leap of faith. I left the comfort and prestige of the Fortune 500 corporate world, cobbled together some start-up funding, and opened Travelogue, Inc.

It was at this point that something became established definitively in my mind: I was going to become a United States citizen. Maybe the thought had always been there, even as far back as when I'd first flown into JFK from London. Nevertheless, there was still the thought in the back of my mind that I could continue my career somewhere in Europe or Asia. But by 1976, the American dream had become *my* dream. This is where I would start my business. This was where I was going to make my home. I applied for permanent residency using my status as an investor, retaining David Carliner, the top immigration attorney in D.C., and maybe the country, to file my application. I was taking no chances.

When I opened my business, I worked hard. I knew that failure was not an option for me. I needed to make it in the

U.S. I felt I was part of an important legacy of first-generation immigrants who came here and succeeded because they had no choice but to do so. America was built by these people and I would often think back to that day in Battery Park when I gazed out at the Statue of Liberty. I drew inspiration from that vision.

Financially, things were tight at the start of the business. I had no banking connections or assets or history of success that could help me secure a solid banking relationship. I ended up living in Farruk's basement to save money, and he and my sister-in-law Rana were most gracious to put me up for this extended stay. One of my challenges was that I didn't know the nuances of the travel industry, so I had to hire some top-notch professionals to help me. But I had learned about sales and marketing, and I knew how to approach my prospective clientele. I struggled at first and would sometimes get depressed, but I shook it off and kept moving. Through it all, I knew I had a winning idea. My niche was overlooked. American Express was not knocking on the doors of companies with a mere half-million-dollar travel budget. Nobody was. We not only knocked, we followed up with close, personal service.

I opened our office a block from K Street, in the heart of D.C., in an area that was heavily populated by lobbyists, lawyers, associations, labor unions, embassies, and multilateral organizations—groups that were always traveling. I installed state-of-the-art automation and a twenty-four-hour, seven-day-a-week, toll-free phone line. I established an airport meet-and-greet service, and developed fully automated, back-office billing and account reconciliation services. To ease cash flow for certain companies, we provided special access to corporate credit facilities.

I hired some crackerjack salespeople and poached some of the leading professionals from the industry.

Little by little, businesses started coming on board and I saw light at the end of the tunnel. By 1978, President Jimmy Carter had signed the Airline Deregulation Act, which is what I'd anticipated when I opened the business. This gave my business even more value. Still, it would take three years before I started breaking even.

I kept working hard and soon enough, brand name companies and institutions began to populate my client roster. One of the early breaks came when we secured the business of Booz Allen Hamilton, the premier U.S. consulting and management company. We snagged them from one of the big travel companies, winning a competitive bid with a dozen other agencies. At the time, Sam Hellier, leading the search committee for Booz Allen, told me we'd no doubt be replaced after two years. It was nothing personal, he explained. It was just that it had been his experience that service has a tendency to drop over time. They'd never had a travel company they were able to stick with. Twelve years later, we would still have Booz Allen Hamilton as a client, quadrupling our business with them in that time.

Landing the Booz Allen Hamilton account was a sweet victory, and confirmation to me that we were doing things right. Soon, Travelogue started winning many major accounts, some of which had a national presence, prompting me to open branches in several cities around the country. One particularly notable account was the up and coming Black Entertainment Television network. In 1980, Robert Johnson co-founded BET and by 1983 it was a full-fledged channel. Bob wasn't happy with his travel provider and decided to interview competing bids for his business. I met him at his then-Georgetown office and he grilled me hard with questions about our capabilities. Finally, he said, "Osman, I think you can do the job." BET was growing and went on to become one of our biggest clients. I found Bob to be an extraordinarily astute businessman, as well as a real gentleman. Eventually, Bob would go on to become America's first black billionaire and I'm humbled to call him my friend to this day. Working for BET was not only a shot in the arm for Travelogue, but a huge boost in confidence for me. To have someone like Bob Johnson put his trust in me meant a lot. At that point, I knew that we could compete with anybody for any size account.

Because Washington, D.C. was the mecca for associations and unions, I knew I needed to branch into the lucrative meetings and conventions business. Accounts such as AFSCME, the American Federation of State, County, and Municipal Employees, with a membership of over a million, would have frequent meetings around the country and an annual convention of up to 10,000 attendees. We arranged special airfares, discounted hotels, transfers, and other services. This became a huge revenue generator for the company. Another avenue I followed was the travel largesse of the federal government. With revenues in the billions, the government travel procurement process was bureaucratic and cumbersome and had definitely been the domain of the big boys. I jumped in and we landed several average-size government accounts and those accounts paved the way for substantially more.

By the late eighties, we were growing at a rapid clip, doubling sales in just a few short years. But I set my sights even higher. I wanted to be a national player. Although I could grow organically, I knew I could move things faster by acquiring and merging other travel companies. My first acquisition was in Baltimore, soon followed by a string of purchases along the eastern corridor. I acquired major competitors in Greensboro, North Carolina, and along the coastline of Florida from South Beach, to Ft. Lauderdale, Boca Raton, and Delray Beach.

One of my most significant acquisitions was a company called TravelNet in Columbus, Ohio in 1994. TravelNet was the precursor of today's online travel. It had jointly collaborated with TWA and they had developed a software program that allowed corporations to explore their airline and hotel options and send their preferences back to TravelNet—all online! This was a remarkably smart idea at the time because the internet was not yet available to the public to make travel arrangements. This was new. I sometimes wonder what would have happened had I not divested my business in 1999 just as the internet was really taking off. Could my company have become a leader in online travel, another Expedia or Travelocity? Who's to say? But I have no regrets. And, besides, I have never seen much value in looking back.

With my core business hitting on all cylinders, I began thinking of ways to diversify. I partnered with a few real estate developers on some of their ventures, mostly building and leasing strip malls from Newport, Rhode Island to Columbia, South Carolina. I'd always been intrigued by real estate and these investments also became a good source of tax shelters. In the early nineties, I became one of the founding investors in a private merchant bank headquartered in D.C.—the Theodore Roosevelt Bank. It was set in a very different atmosphere than the typical bank. The idea was personalized service at a high level. The strategy was to acquire the banking business of local, high net-worth individuals. The bank took off successfully but became a victim of the times, getting caught up in the savings and loan crisis. The regulators clamped down with new guidelines that the Theodore Roosevelt Bank could not meet. Reluctantly, after being in operation for only about two years, we closed. You can't always be successful. Failure, too, is part of life.

During all of those years of entrepreneurship, there were other important developments in my life. It wasn't all business. Back in 1976, at a social function one evening, I had met a young woman. Catherine Pennacchi had recently graduated from Georgetown University, magna cum laude, with a B.S. in language and linguistics, majoring in French. At the time, she was working with a major Algerian oil company as their bilingual executive. She was attractive and smart. She had spent a year abroad at Sorbonne and at the University of Paris and she seemed worldly to me. She was interested in different peoples and cultures. I'd been intrigued by her and I guess she must have seen something in me, too, and we began to date. We saw each other regularly as my business went through its opening fits and starts, and as Travelogue became more established, I began thinking more seriously about our relationship. By 1981, it was becoming clear to me that Catherine was the woman I wanted to spend the rest of my life with.

CHAPTER FIVE

Family

CATHERINE WAS ITALIAN AND CATHOLIC. I was Bengali and Muslim. How could such a relationship work? Would such a relationship be accepted? I'm not going to say there weren't a few misgivings and apprehensions on the parts of both our families. After all, neither family had any real experience in inter-racial, intercultural, interfaith, or, international relationships. Now our families had to face all of those things! For Catherine and me, and for our extended families, our marriage would be, quite literally, a leap of faith.

But as different as, at first glance, we might have appeared, our families shared important values—strong traditional immi-grant values. She was raised as I had been, with an emphasis on family, hard work, and education. Born in Newport, Rhode

Island, she grew up in Mercerville, a New Jersey suburb between Princeton and Trenton, a vibrant, tightknit Italian community where she was surrounded by grandparents, uncles, aunts, siblings, and a plethora of cousins. The kids were encouraged to follow educational paths that had been beyond the financial reach of the parents themselves when they'd been young. In addition to Catherine's academic career at Georgetown and in Paris, her younger brother George's educational background would include a PhD in economics from MIT. Today, he's a professor of finance at the University of Illinois, author of a graduate-level textbook and numerous journal articles, and a popular speaker. Catherine's youngest brother, Bob, would earn his engineering degree from the Stevens Institute of Technology in Hoboken and works today for a petrochemical company in Houston where he is a leader in his field. He's a fun-loving guy who enjoys his food, drinks, and cigars. And when the opportunity presents itself, I enjoy those things right along with him!

Catherine first met my parents in Virginia when they were in town visiting and staying at my brother's house. She was invited for dinner and arrived in conservative dress, bearing a handmade dessert. My parents liked her right away. I met Catherine's parents in D.C. where I took them out to a restaurant in Georgetown. Catherine's father had the latest model Jaguar and I had a new Monte Carlo convertible. We hit it off talking about cars, with me conceding that he had the better one.

Catherine's parents, George and Salvatrice (Sally) Pennacchi were second-generation immigrants. George was originally from Trenton. During World War II, Trenton High let seniors leave school early with a diploma if they enlisted in the service, and so

George, all of seventeen years old, went to fight for his country as a Marine, serving with the Fourth Marine Air Wing and US Marine Corp Group 21. George saw action in the Pacific theater while being based in Guam and, eventually, Okinawa. Guam, a US territory since 1898, had been captured by the Japanese the day after the Pearl Harbor attack. It was retaken by American fighting forces three years later after a fierce battle that lasted from July 21 to August 10, 1944. It then became a base for allied operations, complete with five airfields. Army Air Force B-29 bombers flew in and out as the Allies made further advances in the South Pacific, Japan's military now waning dramatically in strength and numbers. George spent days and nights refueling and rearming the US air fleet.

The Battle of Okinawa would be fiercer still. The Allies attacked on April 1, 1945 in the largest amphibious assault in the Pacific Theater during the war. The battle lasted eighty-two days with 75,000 Allied casualties. George's Fourth Marine Air Wing was stationed there until the end of the war. Among other duties, George had the responsibility of guarding Japanese POWs.

Catherine's mother served, too. Sally worked in administration at the Naval Torpedo Station in Newport during the war. Sally's brother Frank Lozito (Catherine's uncle) went into the service in 1942 and became a B-24 pilot, stationed in Venosa, Italy. On August 10, 1944, he was piloting his bomber, "Miss Fitz," with a crew of nine, targeting the Astro Romano oil refinery in Ploesti, Romania, when his plane was hit by German anti-aircraft fire. The heavily damaged plane made it as far as Yugoslavia. One by one the crew members bailed out while Frank fought to keep the plane airborne. Not until everyone else had safely bailed did Frank himself jump out of the plane. He and his nine crew members were rescued by Yugoslav partisans who hid them for several days until an American C-47 transport plane could slip in, land in a grassy field, and pick them up. All had suffered some degree of injury but all would survive. Frank earned medals for bravery and service, along with a Purple Heart.

I learned all of this as I got to know Catherine's wonderful family. Like me, their roots were elsewhere, but their loyalty and patriotism belonged to the United States of America. Corporal George Pennacchi would be buried with military honors in 2000 at the age of seventy-five in Trenton. Lieutenant Colonel Frank Lozito would pass away in 2017 at the age of ninety-eight and would be buried at Arlington National Cemetery with full military honors befitting a war hero. I was privileged to have known these two members of America's Greatest Generation.

And this, too, was a shared value. Yes, Catherine was Italian and Catholic. Yes, I was Bengali and Muslim. But we were both Americans. Catherine's family could respect my roots as I respected theirs. And if there was anybody that understood how important the American dream was to an immigrant, it was Catherine's Italian family. They'd lived it, too. Further, they understood the difficulties of assimilation, even if you're second-generation. Even if you're fighting for your country. George made corporal by the end of the war, but he spoke of being passed over for a promotion several times because of his Italian heritage. Nobody in Catherine's family seemed interested in promoting the kind of discrimination they themselves had faced. They sensed I was a good fit for her, and that was good enough for them.

When we married, we elected to have two ceremonies. The first, on June 26, 1981, was a small Islamic event officiated by the Imam of the Washington Islamic Center, Dr. Muzammil Siddiqi. The next day was a church ceremony in Trenton officiated by Father Michael Tarro, the cousin of Catherine's mom. That ceremony was followed by an elaborate reception attended by all family members and it was a wonderful demonstration of two different families coming together in faith, peace, and love. Catherine and I danced to Elvis Presley's "Love me Tender." The next day, the party continued in D.C. with us hosting a dinner/dance at a local Pakistani restaurant attended by friends, family, and colleagues. We had a live band and the lead singer was Susan Berenson, an Australian friend of Catherine's from her work. The morning after that, we flew to Hawaii for our honeymoon. Yes, Blue Hawaii!

In the meantime, Catherine and I had bought a heavily wooded piece of land in the heart of McLean, Virginia, about a half-hour commute from my office. We'd bought it with the idea of building our dream home and we hired renowned local architect Joe Boggs who would soon be designing the renovated Filene Center amphitheater at the Wolf Trap National Park for the Performing Arts. Catherine and I both wanted to get away from the conventional brick ranch or colonial-style houses that populated our area of Virginia. We wanted something post-modern and Joe Boggs turned out to be the right guy for us. He designed our residence with tall ceilings and lots of open space and windows. He brought in the light from the outside and made the home feel as though it was a part of the wooded environment in which it rested. Eventually, our home would win awards and be featured in several architectural and design magazines.

We hired Joe after returning from Hawaii and then had to race to finish the house before the arrival of our first child. Omar was born on October 6, 1982. We marveled at this miracle of life. Catherine was completely smitten. I was, too, amazed at the feelings our child produced in me. We were parents now, with hardly an idea as to what that might entail, but we joyfully accepted our new roles. At the time, Catherine was the director of administration and an officer of a cutting-edge software firm with a global reach. She took the standard maternity leave, but when it came time to go back to work, she decided against it. Although it was a huge sacrifice to give up such a promising career, it was not a difficult decision for her. She told me that nothing was more important to her than to raise our new son with her full attention and devotion, and I supported her completely.

On February 8, 1984, we added to the family. Julene was born and now we had a daughter. Julene loved music as a little girl and it's no surprise that music is the path she followed in life. Another daughter, Leila, would come along on January 11, 1989. It was a cold night and I still remember driving Catherine, in an advanced stage of labor, to the hospital. The roads were slick and required caution but our new baby wasn't going to wait. We got to the hospital just in the nick of time, but I don't know who was breathing faster that night, Catherine or me.

Leila was the sensitive one, yet fun-loving. I would drive her to her Montessori school in the mornings when her tiny hand could only grip one of my fingers and we would enjoy small talk. She would hide little notes and drawings in my wallet or suitcase when I traveled for business, which was often. These little gems always made me smile and made the trips less stressful.

And then on November 3, 1992, our youngest was born, another boy. We named him Zachary. The day coincided with the day that Bill Clinton was elected forty-second president of the United States and I took this to be a very good omen. Zack was a calm, lovable kid. Later, when we occupied the ambassador's residence in Fiji, Zack, all of seven years old, would become the darling of the staff. Previous ambassadors were older and with grown children. The staff loved having a child around. Zack brightened up the place, riding his bike around the circular driveway and kicking a soccer ball down the hallways. Staff members took to calling him "Ratu," which is Fijian for "Chief." They even made him a specially tailored "sulu," which is their traditional dress, and they designed it in the Fijian way that reflects that the wearer is the highest of chiefs.

Our respective faiths were important to both Catherine and me, although Catherine's influence on the children in this regard was probably a little heavier than mine. But we recognized both faiths as a family, celebrating holidays like Eid al-Fitr and Eid ul-Azha as well as Christmas and Easter. I followed my father's lead: "We are all people of the Book." The roots of both our traditions were sourced in the legacy of Abraham. And just as I had been encouraged to keep an open mind, I encouraged my children to keep an open mind as well. Neither Catherine nor I would force a religion onto our children. Our goal was to raise them sensitively and intelligently and allow their own inquiring minds to set their respective theological courses.

As they grew, I tried to be there for the children as much as I possibly could, but Catherine was the steady one, the one who made sure that everybody was getting off to school on time in the morning and that everyone's homework had been done.

She was a rock. Neither one of us coddled the kids, but the kids knew they were loved. And they had experiences not often available to other children. I was in the travel business, after all, and that meant affordable trips to faraway places, allowing the kids exposure to different ways of life. By the time our kids were in college, they'd been provided great insight on the world and its peoples and cultures.

We raised four wonderful children, but of course parenting has its share of challenges. Kids don't always do what you want or expect them to. We had our moments, as all parents do. But we are proud that our kids have grown into such terrific adults, each of them unique and each following his or her passion. Omar did his undergraduate studies in Australia and completed his master's in international relations at NYU. Today, he is an international diplomat stationed in Bangkok with a senior position at UNESCAP—the United Nations Economic and Social Commission for Asia and the Pacific. In Catherine's high school yearbook, she had written that she wanted to pursue her higher studies in languages because she'd wanted to work for the U.N. Now, she's fulfilled that dream through the achievements of her son.

Julene, meanwhile, fulfilled my dream of music through her achievements. Not long ago she married Euan Rafferty, a fine Scottish gentleman. The wedding was in the small, picturesque town of Praiano on the idyllic Amalfi coast of Italy. One immediate challenge: we couldn't find an English-speaking priest in this charming village of 2,000 residents. Julene eventually found one in a neighboring town who was happy to come to Praiano and perform the ceremony. Euan brought in Scottish bagpipers to play after the service. After the ceremony, Catherine and

I hosted a dinner reception at a magnificent restaurant with a history that included such guests as Frank Sinatra and Jackie Kennedy. The restaurant was built into a cliff overlooking the Mediterranean, beyond the moonlit waters of which could be seen the lights of Capri. All of Euan's male family members came in their traditional Scottish kilts with bagpipers in tow.

The day before, on Julene's request, and to my great delight, my family held a Bengali-Islamic ceremony that was officiated by my older brother Farruk, with my brother Khaled by his side. All the guests of the following day's church service were invited. My sisters Zereen, Nasreen, and Florin were present and arranged the food, music, readings, and even the attire for everyone—traditional clothing for all to wear, even the staff. There was a spiritual reading on the meaning of the occasion by my niece Farah. Two other nieces, Natasha and Sophie, performed a modern Bollywood dance sequence, which enthralled the guests. Julene was walked to the ceremony under a canopy held by Omar, Zack, and Catherine's two nieces Anna and Alyssa. Euan, in full prince regalia, was escorted in by Catherine's brother Bob and my brother Yousef. All of the events surrounding the wedding were memorable and the scenery—the palms and the groves of lemon and olive trees, with the glistening sea as the backdrop—made the entire visit a magical time for everyone. Today, the happy couple make their home near London.

Leila graduated from the University of Miami's school of business with a bachelor's degree in business administration with concentrations in management and finance. Today, she works in the digital space in media and technology. She hasn't lost her sense of thoughtfulness. For my sixty-fifth birthday, she co-conspired with Catherine to organize a surprise party with most of my relatives and many of my friends. What really made my eyes glisten was the thick scrapbook she'd spent months putting together, complete with nostalgic photographs and poignant notes written by friends and family. I keep that book displayed prominently on our coffee table.

Zack grew up as the athletic one in the family. He played soccer and football. At Langley High, his football career was cut short by a ferocious hit he made on an opponent one night at a home game. Catherine and I watched helplessly from the stands as Zack came off the field, his arm dangling by his side. He'd dislocated his shoulder and would ultimately need a couple of operations to fix it. He was disappointed, naturally, to end his playing days, but I don't mind confessing that Catherine and I were a little relieved. Football is a rough sport.

Zack went on to get his undergraduate degree in environmental and ecological engineering from Purdue University, arch-rival of my beloved Indiana. There was some good-natured ribbing about who was paying tuition, but of course I encouraged his choice nonetheless. Today, we get together to watch the annual Purdue-Indiana football game wearing our respective university colors. Zack works for an investment advisor, working in the mission-related investment field.

The journey with Catherine has been wondrous and amazing. When I'd contemplated marriage back in 1981, well, that seems a hundred years ago in some ways. Yet in other ways, it seems like only yesterday. I remember distinctly that first dance, Elvis crooning "Love me Tender." I remember distinctly our honeymoon to "Blue Hawaii." And I remember something else about those days. Another defining milestone in my life. I was going to become a citizen of the United States. In fact, David

Carliner, my immigration attorney, called me after the wedding with an idea. "Osman," he said, "now that you're married, you don't need to use your investor status for residency. You're the spouse of a U.S. citizen. It's a fast-track. You can have your permanent residency in ninety days."

Without any hesitation, I said, "No thank you, David. I don't ever want anyone thinking that I married Catherine for any purpose other than the real one: I married her for love." We stayed with the investor status. Meanwhile, that love for Catherine has grown many-fold with each addition to our wonderful and blessed family. Catherine has been my moral compass, reminding me by word and by deed to stay humble, be charitable, and live with integrity. Our initial differences, far from being obstacles, have, instead, become beautiful contrasts in a larger, evolving tapestry of growth and love and understanding.

American

THERE WERE ABOUT FORTY OF us in the Alexandria court-house that crisp autumn day, people from all over the world, all of us just moments away from seeing our dreams come true. Catherine was with me. I wore my favorite suit and tie for the occasion and held tightly to the small American flag we were all issued. We stood when the judge entered and we remained standing as he spoke the words that we all repeated in unison:

> I hereby declare, on oath, that I absolutely and entirely renounce and abjure all allegiance and fidelity to any foreign prince, potentate, state, or sovereignty of whom or which I have heretofore been a subject or citizen; that I will support and defend the Constitution and

laws of the United States of America against all enemies, foreign and domestic; that I will bear true faith and allegiance to the same; that I will bear arms on behalf of the United States when required by the law; that I will perform noncombatant service in the Armed Forces of the United States when required by the law; that I will perform work of national importance under civilian direction when required by the law; and that I take this obligation freely without any mental reservation or purpose of evasion; so help me God.

I was struck by the power of this oath, the responsibility that was being conferred upon me. I realized that this is what it meant to be a citizen of this country and I wondered how many Americans, birthed here, who took their citizenship for granted, understood these obligations. Did they know the immense importance of both the privileges and responsibilities that came with being an American? That day, I was taking them "freely without any mental reservation." The sense of duty gave me a sense of belonging. I was now a part of this country. When the judge declared us all naturalized citizens of the United States, I swallowed hard to rid myself of the lump in my throat, then joined in the applause that filled the room. I'd been given permanent resident status two years prior, but that was only a prelude to what I'd coveted ever since I had decided that this country was going to become my home. I wanted to be an American citizen. And on that day, October 17, 1985, I became one.

Since that day, I've thought a lot about becoming a citizen and what it's meant to me. After all, unlike the majority of Americans, the privilege was not conferred upon me at birth; I had to seek it out. Like anything you have to work for, the privilege meant a lot to me. I had a deep sense of what it meant to be an American. America is unlike any place else with respect to its citizenry. You can become a British citizen, but if you're from elsewhere, you can never be an Englishman. You can become a French citizen, but if you're from elsewhere, you can never be a Frenchman. In America, anybody from anywhere, going through the proper channels, can become *an American*. If you're an American, those fifty stars on the flag stand for you as much as they stand for anybody else—from the president on down. This is the promise of the lady who stands on Liberty Island with her torch raised high, the lady I had spied from Battery Park on one of my very first days on U.S. soil.

We had to take a citizenship test before we qualified to take the oath, questions about the history of this country, questions about the Constitution and the Declaration of Independence. I breezed through it. Not because I was especially smart, but because I'd made it a point to study about my new nation. I found its history to be amazing. The brilliance and foresight of the Founding Fathers was astounding to me. I read the Constitution with its beautiful "We The People" preamble and felt exalted by the simplicity of the document, a living instrument that has governed this country since the document's ratification in 1788. I loved the poetry and philosophy of the Declaration: "We hold these truths to be self-evident, that all men are created equal, that they are endowed by their Creator with certain unalienable Rights, that among these are Life, Liberty and the pursuit of Happiness."

After I took the oath, I invalidated my Bangladeshi passport. There would be no such thing as dual citizenship for me, and it was more than just the pledge I'd made in that Alexandria courtroom. To me, dual citizenship seemed like something for somebody who can't make up their mind. A way to split your loyalty so as to hedge your bets. There would be no fence-sitting for me. My allegiance was to one flag.

This was consistent with my thoughts about assimilation. I'd always appreciated the idea of so many cultures coming to America and remaining true to themselves. America has historically allowed this, after all. Encouraged it even. Complete allegiance to the Stars and Stripes has never meant forgetting where you're from. We have the freedom in this country to celebrate all cultures. And our immigrants have given us so much. A list of immigrants who have helped shape this country over the years includes names like Einstein, Pulitzer, Tesla, and Carnegie. More recent immigrants who have proven influential include Madeleine Albright (who would become my boss), Arnold Schwarzenegger, Arianna Huffington, Fareed Zakaria, and thousands more. Former Chairman of the Joint Chiefs of Staff, General John Shalikashvili, overseeing the most powerful army in the world, came to us from Poland. Fazlur Rahman Khan, designer of the Sears Tower, since renamed Willis Tower and the one-time tallest building in the world, was from my own Bangladesh. Did you know Bob Hope and Elizabeth Taylor were both from England or that Irving Berlin was from Russia? Did you know that more than 100 U.S. Nobel winners are immigrants?

From the very beginning, our immigrants have made us stronger and richer. And yet, the real beauty of this land is the many differing cultures coming together into something larger than us all. *E pluribus unum*: out of many, one. In my estimation, diversity means strength, but unity means power. We're a melting pot, a mosaic of ethnicities and theologies and philosophies and political ideas. But, in our best moments, we are also united. Our cultural backgrounds might be different, but our national heritage is a shared one. We all walk the land that those Founding Fathers created for us. It's disconcerting for me when I see people living here as naturalized citizens who hang on too tightly to their past, who don't participate in American traditions, who don't assimilate, who don't even bother to learn the language. If you are a citizen of this country, you must become a real part of it. Citizenship in this great land should never be taken lightly.

None of this means, of course, that a person needs to believe that America is always a perfect country. Our history is full of missteps. But the genius of our Founding Fathers is that our Constitution allows for correction and change and growth. We can right wrongs. If we see an injustice, we can speak up freely about it. This is the beauty of the First Amendment: *Congress shall make no law respecting an establishment of religion or prohibiting the free exercise thereof, or abridging the freedom of speech or of the press, or the right of the people peaceably to assemble and to petition the government for a redress of grievances.* It is our right to participate in our nation's political processes. There are few countries that allow this level of free speech. Indeed, there are countries—Saudi Arabia, China, North Korea, Syria, and many others—where petitioning for "a redress of grievances" can be a life-threatening proposition.

This built-in capacity for peaceful change, this freedom to continually reflect and review, is, perhaps, the best gift our Founding Fathers gave us. It allows the nation to bend without breaking. It's the suspension of Bus USA, the shock absorbers that hold it all together when we hit the inevitable bumpy roads. We bounce around and maybe even come up out of our seats, but we hang on and the vehicle remains intact. Presidents and congressmen and senators and Supreme Court justices come and go, and the nation moves on.

The fact is, most political ideas seem to come into power and then go back out again. Often, it's like the swing of a pendulum. Our governmental structure not only allows for change of thought, it encourages it. If your side lost this election, there will always be another. In 2016, for example, there was much consternation about the presidential election and fear about the new administration. I was invited to speak at George Washington University shortly after the election to discuss contemporary issues with students. I rose to speak and saw angst and anxiety in the students' faces. Many of these kids were foreign and they feared the new administration's negative talk about immigrants. Xenophobia suddenly seemed ubiquitous. The students feared other disagreeable political positions, too, which were now coming into power. They looked beaten and dejected.

"Listen," I said to them, "don't look so solemn! There is nothing wrong with America. This is the same country it's always been. Are you worried about your residency status?" With that, I pulled out my pocket copy of the Constitution and read them the Fourteenth Amendment. I read to them of the rights of naturalized citizens and I read to them the equal protection clause that was written for *all persons* within the United States. "The Constitution has your back," I said. "Look, there are three branches of government. The Founding Fathers were wise. You have nothing to fear and nothing to be down about. *You* are the future of our country. If there is something you don't like, you have the power to change it." Afterward, some of the angst had been replaced by hope. And why not? In America, there is always hope.

In addition to the freedom to participate in this country's governance, we are also free in this land to pursue our own individual hopes and dreams. You can be who you want to be. I have found that there is opportunity enough for all here, and if you play by the rules and work hard, the sky is the limit. Nobody can stop you if you put your mind and set your heart to whatever it is you wish to do. This is the real miracle of this country and, for me, the promise of America has been realized a thousandfold.

It's been more than thirty years since that crisp October day in an Alexandria courthouse, holding that flag with Catherine by my side. We celebrated quietly that night. The day had felt almost sacred to me. My becoming a citizen seemed more than just an accomplishment. It felt like a new beginning, as though I'd somehow been born anew. In a way, I had been. What I became that day changed my life. And the rebirth made me feel proud. Prouder than I had ever felt before. Yes, I was from Bangladesh. East Pakistan, if you want to go back even further, and, yes, of course, my heritage would always be important to me. Bangladesh was my motherland. But the United States was now my homeland. I was now—officially and forever—an American.

CHAPTER SEVEN

"And the Dream Lives On"

IN NOVEMBER OF 1988, I voted as an American for the first time. In fact, it was the first time I had voted in my entire life. If I'd felt like a real part of my new country before, I felt even more so on that day. I was taking advantage of my Constitutional rights and participating in the democratic process. I felt empowered. I felt eight feet tall.

The election I cast my vote in was no less than the presidential election of that year. I chose George H.W. Bush. I liked him. He was following on the heels of Ronald Reagan and the country seemed in fine shape, with a booming economy and a strong defense. As the years went along, however, I found myself beginning to gravitate more toward the social platform of the Democrats. I believed, and still believe, that government has an important role to play in helping people. Whether it's with Medicare, Social Security, or other avenues of assistance and direction, the government must be empowered to take care of its citizenry. That said, the citizenry has its responsibilities, too. We must never become a nation that simply hands people things, or a nation that taxes its people arbitrarily for a greater good that goes undefined. A government's role in the lives of its people must always be weighed carefully.

Reasonable people can disagree about that role, of course, and I can disagree with a Republican stance on this or that issue and still understand and respect it. I hope for the same courtesy on a stance I might take that may be at odds with a Republican position. At our finest, our nation uses our two-party system to find that proper role of government. When we're not so much at our finest, we tend to attack and insult our fellow citizens. I find this extremely troubling. Despite my eventual ideological differences, I became a friend of the Bush family, visiting President George H.W. Bush at the White House along with my family and being treated to a private tour led by none other than First Lady Barbara Bush. By then, I had become good friends with the Bush's son Marvin, brother of George W. and Jeb Bush, and it was he who organized the visit. I even attended George W. Bush's first swearing-in as governor of Texas as a special guest of the family, and supported Jeb Bush's first gubernatorial bid in Florida. You see, we can disagree on the fundamentals, but we can still be agreeable. We all want what's best for our country; we sometimes just have differing opinions of what that is at any given time.

My movement towards the Democratic party soon had me working for and supporting many local, state, and national

Democratic candidates, as well as participating in fundraisers for, and working closely with, the Democratic National Committee. That's the thing about living in Washington, D.C. I imagine if one lives in Hollywood, one can't help but take an interest in the cinema. Well, in Washington, D.C., you can't help but take an interest in politics. It's heavy in the air. It's unavoidable. It's contagious. Before I knew it, I'd become sucked in by the processes of our great democracy, and I wanted to become further involved.

At one DNC fundraiser, held in the large ballroom of a Washington, D.C. hotel, I noticed Senator Ted Kennedy. I'd never forgotten his involvement with the nation of Bangladesh during its turbulent beginning and, of course, I remembered that it was he who had led the airline deregulation hearings, so pivotal for me at the start of my travel business. Senator Kennedy, without being aware of it, had been a huge influencing factor in my life, and I knew I had to meet him.

I introduced myself and the senator smiled that famous Kennedy smile and began asking me questions about my background, perking up when I talked about my motherland. He took a sincere interest in what I had to say and we talked for some time about a range of issues. Finally, he told me I was welcomed to come see him and his staff at any time. "Please keep in touch with me," he said, shaking my hand and bidding me a goodnight.

I took him up on his offer a week or so later and I also began to see him at other Democrat functions. We would always talk and, before long, we formed a friendship. Kennedy was living in McLean, Virginia at the time, as was I, and he came over a few times, once to play tennis.

Kennedy had served as a Massachusetts senator since 1962 and, for the most part, had never really been seriously challenged at re-election time. In fact, one election year, he turned to me and joked, "I'm running hard. I'm running scared. I'm running unopposed!" That all changed in 1994. A youthful, successful businessman by the name of Mitt Romney decided to throw his hat into the ring. Romney ran as a Washington outsider with strong family values. Two months before the election, the polls were neck and neck. Romney had money, too. Despite the general opinion that the Kennedy wealth was endless, the senator struggled that year. He called a lot of people for help, including me.

I offered to host a fundraiser in my home, which he gratefully accepted. Then I suggested we change the venue and hold it at his house. I'd host and take care of all of the details, but it seemed to me as if we could make a stronger impression on our guests if the dinner was held at Kennedy's own place. He agreed and the event turned out to be a big success. He took guests around his home, walking them into his library where a piano sat that JFK had played. I noticed a plaque on the wall from Bangladesh, a gift in appreciation for his work, no doubt, with a quote from Nobel laureate Rabindranath Tagore.

At one point, I made a speech. I talked about how I'd come to this country from Bangladesh and what the promise of America had meant to me. I talked about how others come here for that same promise, from Vietnam, China, India, Central America, Africa, everywhere. "Why are they here?" I said, glancing over at the senator. "Because of people like you. You have spent your career helping the underdog, fighting for the underprivileged, and giving voice to the voiceless." The speech moved the senator.

Afterward, his wife Vicki approached me and confided that she'd never seen him quite so emotional before. My friendship with Kennedy became even stronger that night. And, of course, he defeated Romney in the senatorial election that November.

We continued to keep in touch through the nineties, even though he eventually moved to the posh Kalorama neighborhood of D.C. to be closer to the Hill. He was getting tired of the commute. And then in 2004, Senator Kennedy became very active in the candidacy of John Kerry, the party nominee for president. Kerry was the junior senator of Massachusetts and Kennedy, the senior senator, had been something of a mentor to him. I was active in Kerry's campaign, too, but Kennedy got me even more deeply involved, bundling me with Congressman Mike Honda from California, and Governor Gary Locke from the state of Washington. Honda had an interesting background. As an infant, he'd been put in an Japanese internment camp with his parents at the start of World War II. Locke had been the first governor in the continental United States of East Asian descent. Later, he'd be commerce secretary and then ambassador to China. Our job? To campaign extensively throughout Ohio, Michigan, and Pennsylvania. Census data showed a preponderance in this area of Asian-Americans and other minorities. We needed to mobilize them to action.

One especially interesting stop along the way was the small township of Hamtramck, Michigan. Hamtramck had been a virtual magnet for immigrants, especially Bangladeshis. In fact, the 2000 census showed that 19.7 percent of the population had come from Bangladesh. Later, in 2015, Hamtramck would boast the first majority Muslim city council in the United States. Needless to say, I was very welcomed there.

On one of the last days of our campaign, we held a huge event in the basketball arena of Ohio State University in Columbus. The place was packed and by the enthusiastic crowd, you might have mistaken the atmosphere for an NCAA Final game. We each gave short speeches and then took questions from the largely student audience. One of the questions directed at Governor Locke was about 9/11 being, in this student's words, "a response to our failed and biased Mideast policies." I asked the governor if I might step in to answer the question. I felt a Muslim ought to be heard and Governor Locke kindly obliged.

I stood and spoke directly to the student. "No matter how good or bad our policies have been," I began, "and no matter how flawed our leadership may be, nothing—nothing—justifies such a heinous and dastardly attack on our soil, on our city, and on our innocent people. Did you know that many amongst the 3,000-plus killed that day were Arabs, Muslims, and other minorities? All Americans should condemn that attack. There can never be *any* justification for such an act of terror." My answer was met with applause and cheering. Later, I would reflect on the idea that I had been in that arena in the first place. If I said something that might have been meaningful for people to hear, then my involvement in U.S. politics was worthwhile. I could make a difference. This person from Dhaka, who hadn't voted until he was thirty-eight, was able to influence the American conversation, in however small a way. What can be more democratic and American than that?

Late in that campaign season, I attended the grand finale fundraiser for John Kerry at the Chelsea Pier in New York City. Omar was in the grad program at NYU at the time and I brought him along. There were at least a couple of thousand people at the fundraiser and when Omar and I came in, we had trouble finding our table. Kennedy's chief of staff, Tom Lopach, spotted us and came over saying, "Stay here, Osman, we'll find you a place." Shortly after that, I noticed Senator Kennedy waving to me from the front table where he was seated. People were taking their seats, so I waved back as Omar and I slowly made our way through the room looking for our spot. But then I noticed the senator wasn't waving *to* me, he was waving me towards him, beckoning us to the front table. The next thing I knew, we were sitting next to Caroline Kennedy, daughter of JFK and niece to Ted.

I'd never met Caroline before and found her delightful. She asked Omar about NYU. He told her he was studying international relations and she told him not to overlook public service. "And have you thought about foreign service?" she said. To me, she asked about Fiji, knowing that, by then, I'd served as ambassador there. As it happened, Fiji is where she and her husband had gone for their honeymoon. "It was one of the best times of our lives," she said. We traded many stories about Fiji and Fijian culture. About ten years later, Caroline would become an ambassador herself, to Japan.

Senator Kennedy was re-elected in 2006 for his eighth full term and in January of 2007, I found myself in the Capitol building for the Senate swearing-in ceremonies. People were milling about in the hallways and at one point, Senator Kennedy turned to me and pointed down the corridor towards one of the younger senators, a tall, African-American gentleman who had been elected to his first term in 2004.

"Osman," Kennedy said, "I think that gentleman is looking for me. Please, go get him, will you? He's our senator from Illinois. Name is Barack Obama."

I did as Kennedy said and retrieved the Illinois senator. "Senator Obama? I'm Osman Siddique. Kindly follow me, please. Senator Kennedy is waiting to receive you."

"Of course," he said.

How could I have known then that I was directing around a future president? I knew that these two lawmakers had business to attend to, so I excused myself, but not before Senator Kennedy had formally introduced me to Senator Obama as "my favorite ambassador." I knew it was hyperbole, but that's the way the senator was, never lacking for a compliment.

That would turn out to be Senator Kennedy's final term. In May of 2008, after two seizures, he was diagnosed with a brain tumor. Despite surgery and treatment, his condition steadily worsened. Nevertheless, in August of that same year, against doctors' orders, he made a stunning appearance at the Democratic National Convention in Denver, the convention where that freshman senator I'd met in the hallway in the Capitol just a few short years prior, was set to receive the party nomination for president.

As it happened, I had been a supporter of Hillary Rodham Clinton. Ted Kennedy knew this. We had talked about it in early January of that year, before his health issues, at his home in Kalorama. He had invited me by and I remember Vicki was traveling at the time, forcing the senator to fend for himself. He managed to fix us a couple of gin and tonics, but searched in vain for the limes. We laughed about it, about our mutual dependence on our better halves. Kennedy hadn't endorsed anyone at the time, but he knew that later that night, I was heading to Hillary's house for a fundraiser. "You're doing the right thing," he said to me, knowing of the relationship I'd had with the

Clintons by then. "Have a good time. But keep your powder dry." I had a sense just then that Hillary wasn't going to be the beneficiary of the senator's endorsement. Sure enough, two weeks later, Senator Kennedy threw his weight behind Barack Obama.

Now, at the convention, I was fortunate to be seated near the Kennedys. Caroline was there. So was Maria Shriver and others. Everybody was anticipating Ted's speech. With his health condition, there were jitters, of course, but there needn't have been. The senator hit it out of the park that night, saying, "This November, the torch will be passed again to a new generation of Americans…The work begins anew. The hope rises again. And the dream lives on." The crowd was electrified. This man had been in a hospital just the night before. I looked over at the Kennedy family and there wasn't a dry eye. In fact, that evening in the convention center, there were few dry eyes.

I went to my hotel room that night energized by the convention while at the same time harboring a sense of melancholy. I knew the state of health Ted was in and I thought to myself that I probably would never see him again. I slipped into bed just as my phone received a text. It was from Kennedy's staff. "The senator would like to invite you to a breakfast tomorrow at 9:00 a.m." Then it gave the name of the restaurant along with explicit instructions not to disclose the breakfast or its whereabouts. My melancholy turned to excitement. One more chance to see the senator.

That next morning, there were probably a hundred friends, family, and loyal supporters of the senator in attendance at his breakfast. I took my seat at a table where Congressman Barney Frank and his chief of staff were seated, but soon I heard a booming voice. "Ambassador! Ambassador! Osman! Osman! Why are you sitting over there?" Of course it was Senator Kennedy. "Come sit with me!" Just like at the Chelsea Pier. This time, there were fewer people and the booming voice meant that all eyes were now focused on me. With a little embarrassment, I excused myself from the company of Congressman Frank and made my way to Kennedy's table where he had some rearranging done to open up a seat next to his. Senator Chris Dodd was at the table along with Howard Dean, the Chairman of the Democratic National Committee; and Thomas Menino, the mayor of Boston. The conversation was absorbing that morning and I felt humbled to be in the presence of such important figures.

That would be the last time I would ever see Senator Kennedy in person. In August of 2009, he passed away at his home in Hyannis Port, Massachusetts. He was seventy-seven and had spent most of his life in public service, championing the causes he felt were important. For me, he inspired not just an interest in politics, but involvement in our democratic process. For that, I will always be grateful. Of his friendship, I will always be proud.

CHAPTER EIGHT

1996

BACK IN 1992, ON THE day my son Zack was born, William Jefferson Clinton was elected president. I had only recently started getting involved in the political process. It had been just four short years before then that I had cast my first-ever vote. But by 1996, I was all in. And that meant helping out in whatever way I could to make certain that we were going to have another four years of Bill Clinton in the White House. The competition was formidable: Senate Majority Leader Bob Dole. And he wasn't the only one. Texan billionaire Ross Perot was back again, having run unsuccessfully as an independent in 1992. Nevertheless, he'd managed to garner nineteen percent of the popular vote in '92 and was not a force to be taken lightly. The general thinking was that Perot was going to siphon off more Republican voters than Democratic voters, but who could really say? Perot was something of a loose cannon and there was an air of unpredictability during the entire campaign season.

I had seen Clinton in various fundraisers and other party events, but I'd never actually been formally introduced to him. In March of 1996, I finally had the chance to not only meet him, but to offer him my perspective on things. I was invited, as part of a group of fifteen key supporters, to dine with the president at the famous Hay-Adams Hotel in Washington, D.C. We were all seated around a very large, rectangular dining table. The president came in a little late and sat down two people from me. In between us was Marvin Shanken, publisher of *Wine Spectator* and *Cigar Aficionado* magazines. Small talk was made around the table and then Senator Christopher Dodd, general chairman of the party at the time, asked each of us to stand and speak for two minutes, to introduce ourselves to the president and express whatever might be on our minds.

The problem was, I was to the president's right and Dodd started with the person to the president's left. There were thirteen speakers before me. Of course, none of them limited themselves to two minutes. By the time it was my turn to stand and speak, time was running out. Dodd said, "Osman, I'm afraid we have to cut it off here. The president is running late and I'm sure you understand."

Naturally, although greatly disappointed, I was ready to concede my time. But before I could reply, President Clinton interjected and said, "No, Chris, I want to hear what Osman has to say. Please let him speak." It was a gesture I will never forget. The president was, indeed, running late, but nevertheless wanted to take the time to hear from a supporter whom he barely knew. I was humbled.

"Thank you, Mr. President," I said as I stood, nervous yet somehow confident at the same time. I knew what I wanted to say. "First of all, I want to congratulate you. Last year, we witnessed a horrific terrorist act on our own soil. But within hours of the Oklahoma City bombing, you stepped in with the voice of reason, admonishing people not to jump to conclusions. At a time when most Americans were assuming the crime had to have been carried out by Middle Eastern terrorists, a time when even innocent American people of Muslim faith or Middle Eastern descent were looked at with suspicion, you advised that we wait for the facts to present themselves. Sure enough, the perpetrator was soon found to be a terribly misguided American."

The president nodded warmly and I continued, "Mr. President, I would also like to ask that you pass along my heart-felt thanks to the First Lady." With this, the president perked up even more. "Mrs. Clinton organized the very first ceremony ever held at the White House for the breaking of the fast of Ramadan. In this largely Judeo-Christian country of ours, the First Lady's inclusion of this significant event was nothing less than momentous. And very much appreciated." With that, I noticed the president jotting down something in a little notebook, a reminder, I supposed, to pass my sentiments to Mrs. Clinton.

After the dinner, each guest, per custom, offered a gift to the president. Someone gave him a set of golf clubs. Shanken, naturally, presented him with a box of cigars. Me, I gave the president a copy of John Naisbitt's book *Megatrends Asia*. He shook my hand and thanked me and handed the book to an aide and I assumed that would be the end of it. But two months later, I attended a fundraiser at the home of Baltimore mayor Kurt Schmoke. President Clinton was there, shaking hands with everybody in a receiving line. The line moved quickly as the president wanted to get to everyone, but when it was time to shake my hand, he held onto it just a little longer.

"Osman," he said, "I read that book you gave me. I was especially interested in Naisbitt's take on the modernization of China." And then he began to expand on points in the book that made me realize that he wasn't just being polite with me. He had clearly read the book. I was equal parts flattered and impressed. I knew that in that two-month period since our dinner at the Hay-Adams Hotel, the president must have shaken thousands of hands. Somehow he'd remembered me, and he'd also made time to delve into Naisbitt's book. Over time, I came to learn that Bill Clinton was a voracious reader and one who retained what he read.

In May, there was a huge gala fundraising event at the Marriott in Stamford, Connecticut. Earlier, President Clinton had picked up the backing of some 2,500 corporate executives who endorsed his administration as being favorable for the nation's business climate and they were all there that night. I attended with a dozen corporate donors whose support for the president I had worked hard to garner. I had twice that many checks from additional supporters.

Entering the room, I noticed an especially high level of security. This was not surprising. Clinton wasn't just a candidate; he was a sitting president. Once through security, everyone in my contingent was presented with a ticket and badge that allowed access and gave the particular table assignment. We began moving toward our table when two stone-faced secret service agents pulled me aside, much to the puzzlement and concern of my guests. Then the agents ushered me away. I turned back toward my group as I followed the agents and shrugged helplessly, wondering if I should shout to them to get me an attorney. Where was I being taken? What kind of interrogation was I facing? *What had I done?*

We walked through a cordoned-off section that led to a corridor which, in turn, led to a dais at the very front of the large hall. My concerns lifted as I was further led to a raised table where four other people were seated along with none other than the guest of honor: President Clinton himself. I was flattered and humbled once again. Millionaire and even billionaire CEOs were sitting at their tables, no doubt wondering who this guy was who'd been invited to sit next to the president.

I thanked the president for thinking of me and we made some small talk, but I could tell his attention was elsewhere. It was a big night and before long the speeches began. George David, CEO of United Technologies extolled the president's efforts at keeping inflation down as well as interest rates. He praised his foreign policy work to raise U.S. exports. And he lauded the president for focusing on education and research. Businessperson Carolyn Staddler from Marietta, Georgia, Speaker Newt Gingrich's district, introduced the president to her fellow CEOs by telling a moving story of her difficult life and eventual success. Her childhood had been hard. She'd lost her parents at the age of eleven. She was married by fifteen and pregnant at sixteen, the latter getting her thrown out of school. She lost her husband when she was twenty-six. Nevertheless, she ultimately started her own paving business, very slowly building it. She almost went bankrupt during the 1990-'91 recession. "Then President Clinton was elected," she said. She didn't vote for him in 1992, she admitted, but wasn't going to make that mistake a second time. Over the course of Clinton's first term, Carolyn's business had become stronger and stronger. "Things are better for me, for my company, and for my employees," she said, capturing the thoughts of many in that room in simple, human terms. *Things were better.* What better raison d'etre did any of us need?

When Clinton ultimately spoke, he said he was glad we had proven that the Democratic party was not the party of big government, hearkening back to his earlier theme that the era of big government was over. The message greatly resonated with the men and women in that room that night. A record $2.3 million was raised and the gala felt less like a campaign fundraiser and more like a celebration.

That campaign season, I worked hard at the grassroots level to mobilize voters and I worked closely with the DNC finance team. At the Democratic National Convention in Chicago, I was asked to interact with some minority delegates and to lead different sub-groups on discussions of policy. I was tasked, as well, with communicating our message to some of the international media that were present, such as Al Jazeera and others.

Chris Dodd made a nomination speech at the convention asserting that President Clinton "has the courage, the vision, and the commitment to bring all Americans together, to the threshold of a new century." To great applause, he concluded, "The choice, my fellow citizens is yours. We're here tonight proud to offer you our choice. I proudly place in nomination before this convention and this country, the name of America's president: William Jefferson Clinton!"

President Clinton's re-nomination speech was powerful and eloquent. He spoke of the administration's success over the prior four years. "We have pursued a simple but profound strategy," he said. "Opportunity for all, responsibility from all, a strong, united American community." He talked about the tone he wanted to set for the campaign against Bob Dole and Ross Perot. "I will not attack them personally, or permit others to do it in this party if I can prevent it. My fellow Americans, this must be a campaign of ideas, not a campaign of insults. The American people deserve it." Then he added: "I love and revere the rich and proud history of America, and I am determined to take our best traditions into the future. But with all respect, we do not need to build a bridge to the past, we need to build a bridge to the future, and that is what I commit to you to do." Finally, hearkening back to his campaign four years earlier, he concluded: "My fellow Americans, after these four, good, hard years, I still believe in a place called Hope, a place called America."

The president won with 49.2 percent of the popular vote to Dole's 40.7 percent and Perot's 8.4 percent. It was a virtual landslide with the electoral vote: 379 to 159 to 0. Clinton became the first Democrat since Franklin Delano Roosevelt to win back-to-back elections.

I was proud to have been of service. At one point, Chris Dodd asked me to his office and presented me with a hand-signed copy of the nomination speech he'd made at the convention: "To Osman Siddique – Thank you for all you have done for me. I'm grateful."

But that wasn't the only call I received to someone's office. As it happened, back on that night at the Hay-Adams Hotel where I had first been formally introduced to the president, I'd met someone very important. After the dinner, several of us were milling about. I was having a nice discussion with Julien Studley, a famous and highly successful commercial real estate broker in Manhattan, when I felt a tap on my shoulder. Turning, I came face to face with Bob Nash, Director of White House Personnel, one of the first African-Americans to be appointed to that position. Bob Nash and President Clinton went way back, all the way back to Arkansas where Bob had initially worked for him as senior executive assistant for economic development while Clinton was governor.

Bob had a broad smile and a warm demeanor. "Sorry to interrupt," he said in his distinctive Arkansas drawl and handing me his card. "Osman, I'd appreciate it if you would please call me. I'd like to set up a visit with you." I assured him I would, not knowing what a meeting with the personnel director of the White House might lead to, but knowing that it was a meeting I could not for a moment consider passing up.

CHAPTER NINE

Bula!

United States Department of State
Washington, D.C. 20520
June 12, 1998

Dear Mr. Siddique:

The White House has advised me that the President has selected you to serve as the Ambassador to Fiji, to the Republic of Nauru, to the Kingdom of Tonga and to Tuvalu. Sincere congratulations.

[...]

Sincerely,
Sharon C. Bisdee
Chief, Presidential Appointments Staff

THIS LETTER CAME ON A beautiful summer day along with a bunch of other mail—bills, circulars, solicitations for charities, all the usual. Rifling through the stack, I stopped immediately when I saw the DOS return address. Then I dumped the rest and carefully opened the envelope.

The appointment was expected, but it still gave me a thrill to see it in official print. Nevertheless, I remained calm and composed, reading the letter a couple of times before walking it over to Catherine and asking her to read it. She scanned it quickly and immediately reached for the World Atlas, Google still being years away. Of course, we both knew about Fiji and Tonga. Fiji was the largest of the Pacific island groups both in terms of land mass and population, and Tonga was the only one that still boasted the title "Kingdom." But we knew very little about Nauru and Tuvalu, almost nothing of their proximity and location and of course their relevance to my appointment. But we would learn. We would learn much about all of these beautiful nations.

The ambassadorial appointment started with that introduction by Bob Nash, handing me his business card at the Hay-Adams and telling me to call him. Of course I did so and we met in his office at the White House shortly after that. Bob told me that in his second term, President Clinton was going to be looking for new members of his administration that would help reflect a cross-section of real Americans, people from different backgrounds and ethnicities, including American Muslims. Was I interested? I told him yes, of course, and we agreed to keep in touch.

Now, as it happens, all of this time, the White House had its eyes on me. By then, because of my profile in the business community and my stature within the Democratic party, I had served as a member of the U.S. delegation to the first Hemispheric Trade and Commerce Forum in Denver, having been invited by Ron Brown, the Secretary of Commerce. I had also served as a presidential delegate to the first White House Conference on Travel and Tourism where industry leaders and policymakers were called together to map out long-term strategies for job creation and export growth. In June of 1996, after my White House meeting with Bob Nash, I was called to serve as a member of the National Democratic Institute's International Observer Delegation to the Seventh Bangladesh Parliamentary Elections, the only Bangladeshi-American in the delegation. What I didn't see until later was that these appointments were essentially auditions, tests of my communication, leadership, and relational skills. I accepted them at face value, never realizing there was a thought in the White House that I might be suited for something bigger.

Bob and I kept in touch before and after the election, and I would see him often at social occasions, including a beautiful White House Christmas dinner that Catherine and I were invited to in December of 1996. It was a wonderful evening of food and dancing in the East Room with the president and first lady. The Marine Corps Band provided the music and the night was magical. Throughout 1997, Bob and I stayed in touch. He would feel me out on my intentions while at the same time gathering more background information on me. I told him at one point that, with my experience and background, I felt I could best serve the president in a role related to international affairs. But of course I made it clear to him that it was for the president to decide.

Toward the end of 1997, Bob called to tell me that Don Gevirtz, ambassador to Fiji, Tonga, Nauru, and Tuvalu, was retiring from his post for personal reasons. The position seemed like a good fit, Bob said. I knew a little about Fiji. I knew that there were some race problems, a divide between Indo-Fijians and ethnic Fijians. I felt my interpersonal skills could be of use. With my business background, I felt I could help in bringing trade to Fiji, too. I told Bob that if that's the place the president needed me, that's the place I'd go. Bob mentioned a consideration about the position that humbled me: I would be the first-ever Muslim-American to serve as an ambassador. I would also come to learn that, as the head of an embassy, I would be the first person from the Indian subcontinent to serve as a U.S. Chief of Mission.

I only briefly mentioned the opportunity to Catherine. I knew there were a lot of hurdles to clear for an ambassadorship. For one thing, I knew I wasn't the only candidate. There were at least a dozen others being considered for the position. And then there would be a comprehensive vetting process. Just how comprehensive, I would soon find out. After all that would come the Senate confirmation hearings. Telling Bob I was interested was only the first step in a very long journey.

The journey got underway in earnest one evening in the Oval Office. Years later, long after we had both finished serving the president, Bob Nash would tell me that it happened like this: he entered the office to see President Clinton sitting at his desk apparently studying something very carefully, scarcely aware that Bob was standing in front of him. Finally, he looked up and noticed. Bob handed him a folder and said, "For your final authorization for the ambassador position to Fiji, Mr. President."

Clinton started perusing the files of candidates, a strong collection of people with diverse and qualified backgrounds. About halfway through, he paused at my file and pulled it out and handed it to Bob. "Don't you want to look at the rest?" asked Bob. President Clinton merely shook his head. With what I can only imagine was a leap of faith by the president, my journey had begun.

The clearance process was tedious and frustrating, but I understood why it was necessary. Ambassadors of the United States are, first and foremost, personal representatives of the president and commander-in-chief. I think it was Richard Nixon who once mused that granting an ambassadorship is the closest our nation comes to bestowing someone with a knighthood. There are seemingly endless personal and general background checks, ethics investigations, financial disclosures including assets and income verifications, legal clearances, investigations of campaign contributions, and more. The FBI, State Department, and other related agencies take a deep dive into one's life history, making sure the candidate can answer any and all questions from the Senate Foreign Relations Committee, plus get acceptance by the host country.

There were no shortcuts to the process. The requests for documentation and corroborations were incessant, as was the need for oral defenses of various queries. My accountants and legal counsels were on twenty-four-hour standby. I divested all of my holdings and interests in my companies, terminated all relationships with other business interests, and resigned from all board and advisory positions. I didn't want to have any conflicts with my new assignment. Briefly, I considered putting the business into a blind trust and coming back to lead it after my service in Fiji would end. I had a good team in place and I knew I could trust them to keep it going while I'd be gone. In the end, however, I decided that I wanted to start with a clean slate and be focused one hundred percent on the job at hand.

But even after I'd done all of that, an ethics official at the State Department called one day asking about a few shares of Boeing stock that I happened to own. Why? Because Air Fiji was in negotiations with Boeing to enhance their existing fleet. My ownership of those few shares represented a conflict of interest. I offloaded the shares immediately.

Finally cleared by the State Department, I was officially nominated by President Clinton on May 27, 1999, eleven months after that letter had arrived from Sharon Bisdee. At that point, the host nation had its concerns. Because of the race divisions in Fiji, the government of Prime Minister Sitiveni Rabuka didn't quite know what to make of an Asian-American ambassador. Communications within the nation's leadership revealed their uneasiness with granting what's known in diplomatic affairs as "agrément," meaning their official acceptance of me. When the White House got wind of this, they pursued the matter with the Rabuka government in no uncertain terms. They made it clear that the president stood firm on my appointment, letting them know that by withholding their agrément, Fiji would risk not having an ambassador for the remainder of the president's term, as well as other possible ramifications. When it came to issues concerning race, President Clinton was uncompromising. And when it came to race reconciliation in Fiji, he admonished Rabuka's government to "Let America lead the way." Fiji soon accepted my appointment and my nomination then headed for the Senate Foreign Relations Committee.

I prepared thoroughly for the hearing, studying and getting briefed on all policy aspects of the region relevant to the countries I would serve. The "Murder Board" set up for me by the Department of State held true to its nickname. The chairman of the Foreign Relations Committee was Senator Jesse Helms from North Carolina, a no-nonsense kind of a guy known for putting several presidential nominees on ice. Most recently, he had held up the nomination of William Weld, Republican governor of Massachusetts, as ambassador to Mexico. Helms was also a Republican, but a very staunch, conservative one. He didn't care for Weld's more liberal support of medical marijuana and other social policy positions. Weld had resigned his governorship in 1997 to take the ambassador position, but Helms essentially ground the nomination process to a halt and Weld never did get the job.

Fortunately, my nomination process went a lot smoother. Senator Helms stayed pretty much out of it, his attention presumably on other staunchly conservative issues. The subcommittee chair for my region (East Asia and the Pacific) was Republican Senator Richard Lugar from Indiana and the ranking member was Democratic Senator Joe Biden from Delaware. Catherine and all four of the kids were with me at the hearing. It was open to the public and I was amazed at the number of spectators who had come. I was honored to be introduced to the committee by the senior Republican senator from Virginia, John Warner. His introduction was brief but heartwarming. He said that as a fellow Virginian, he was proud of my nomination.

In my opening remarks, I took the opportunity to thank the president for honoring me with the nomination and I thanked the committee for its considerations. I talked about the freedom and opportunity we have in America, where every person from any background can strive to reach as high a goal as he or she desires. On policy issues, I congratulated Fiji on the free and fair national elections that had taken place that year, marking the restoration of full democracy following the military coup of 1987 and subsequent political tension between the ethnic Fijians and the Indo-Fijians. I called it Fiji's democratic renaissance, which, naturally, the United States strongly supported. I also recognized Fiji and Tonga's contribution to U.N. peacekeeping missions. The presence of our Peace Corps in Tonga was a further reminder of our commitment and resolve toward the development of the nations of the region. I concluded by committing myself, if confirmed, to being a good steward of the American taxpayers' interests and a prudent and conscientious manager of the public trust.

Senator Lugar asked several pertinent questions and, at one point, expressed that as an alumnus of Indiana University he wished me all the best. Senator Biden likewise asked me some important questions and ended lightheartedly expressing a desire to visit Fiji for some sailing and diving. I would get to know Senator Biden a little better in later years. In 2008, during his run for Democratic Presidential nomination, I would attend a fundraiser on his behalf held in an opulent suite at FedEx Field for a Washington Redskins game and hosted by the Real Estate Roundtable of Washington, D.C. Zack was with me, sixteen years old at the time. While I was discussing politics with some of the guests, including the Senator's son Beau,

I looked over to see Senator Biden in an animated conversation with Zack about the game, each with their own strong opinions about this play or that play. Such was the common touch of this leader and statesman, and the picture of the senator devoting time and attention to a sixteen-year-football enthusiast would be indelibly imprinted in my mind. Not long afterwards, Joe Biden would end his campaign and be chosen by Barack Obama as his vice-presidential running mate.

My hearing ended and not long afterward, on August 5, 1999, the United States Senate unanimously voted to confirm me as the next United States Ambassador to the Republic of Fiji, the Republic of Nauru, the Kingdom of Tonga, and the nation of Tuvalu.

It was good to have the entire ordeal behind me. It had been quite a disruption for me and my family and it's easy to understand why some good people may be reluctant to go through such an arduous process. In a sense, however, we were still going through it. I was confirmed, but now came the disruption of the move itself. This was not an easy time on the home front. It was tumultuous, chaotic, and a bit emotionally challenging. The kids, ranging from six years to sixteen, had never known any other place but their existing home in McLean. And now they were on the verge of being uprooted from their schools, cousins, friends, and social circuits. Why on earth live in Fiji? Catherine and I were sympathetic to their concerns but firm on our resolve that moving to Fiji was the only choice they had. Reluctantly, they acquiesced and the process of dismantling our household with packers, storage people, and visitors running all over our home began.

Catherine had already been on top of it. We'd had a large collection of art and antiques, not to mention our normal household possessions. Some of our possessions we'd take, but most would be left behind. The job of sorting it all out and getting it ready for either shipping or storage was both extensive and elaborate. While I'd been busy with my clearance and confirmation process, Catherine had to bear the brunt of organizing the dismantling of our household. It was a huge task that she undertook single-handedly. It drained her strength and energy, but somehow she made our exit as smooth as possible. For this, I will always owe her a world of gratitude.

My swearing-in ceremony was set for August 17, 1999. I decided that I would take my oath on the Holy Quran and requested the protocol officer at State to arrange for it. As Catherine and I were getting in the car to leave for the State Department on the morning of the swearing-in, I asked Catherine where her Bible was. Puzzled, she said, "Why? I'm not being sworn in." I told her that I wanted to take my oath on both my Quran and her Bible, telling her that I could have not come this far without her prayers, love, and support. She had been with me every step of the way in every aspect of my life and career. Plus, I was reminded of what my father told me: "We are all people of the book." Hurriedly, Catherine went back inside, retrieved her Bible, and away we sped, onto George Washington Parkway, across the Roosevelt Bridge, turning onto Constitution Avenue, with the Lincoln Memorial to our right, and finally coming to a stop at the U.S. Department of State.

The Department of State is sometimes known affectionately as "Foggy Bottom," because of it being located in the neighborhood of the same nickname, a low-lying marshy area on the banks of the Potomac River historically susceptible to fog. But there was no fog on that hot August day. Just sunshine that matched my ebullient mood.

Upon arrival, I was directed to a special underground parking area where I was received by the protocol officer and a few other staffers from the bureau. But I was concerned to see the protocol officer looking pale and nervous. "Is something wrong?" I asked him. Looking down he said that he and his co-workers had desperately been looking for a copy of the Quran, scouring every office and library, but to no avail. I laughed and pulled him toward me said, "It's okay. I brought my own, one that my father passed on to me." At that, the blood came back to the poor officer's face.

The swearing-in took place at the grand Benjamin Franklin Hall at State, packed for the occasion. I was told that besides envoys and emissaries from various Middle Eastern and South Asian countries, they had to make arrangements for a large contingent of international media, along with their heavy cameras and equipment. Many members of our family were present that day, too, along with friends and colleagues. Deputy Secretary, Ambassador Tom Pickering, officiated the proceedings as I placed my hand on the Quran and Bible held together by Catherine. Then I was led through the oath: "I, Osman Siddique, do solemnly swear that I will support and defend the Constitution of the United States against all enemies, foreign and domestic; that I will bear true faith and allegiance to the same; that I take this obligation freely, without any mental reservation or purpose of evasion; that I will well and faithfully discharge the duties of the office on which I am about to enter.

So help me God." It felt almost spiritual to be reciting these words, which seemed sacred to me. I thought of my parents and wished they could have been there.

Secretary Pickering welcomed me to my new position and extolled my virtues as an entrepreneur and politician. He reminded the audience of my modest beginnings in this country and encouraged others to follow my example. I was overwhelmed and humbled by the ceremony and the historical implications. I said a few words, managing to convey my feeling that the miracle of America is that if you work hard and play by the rules, you can reach your dreams. Then I expressed my gratitude for the many people who helped make the occasion possible.

Within a couple of weeks, we were all packed and ready to leave but not before more rounds of consultations and long goodbyes. Finally, we boarded our flight and took off for Fiji, but with one more stop along the way: Honolulu. Yes, blue Hawaii! Hawaii always lifted our hearts and spirits. Catherine and I had celebrated our honeymoon there, after all. In one of our very favorite places in the world, the children always enjoyed snorkeling, jet-skiing, and paragliding, and we all found the flora and fauna distinctive and refreshing. I had yet to bump into Elvis on Waikiki Beach, but we still loved the place. This time, however, our visit wasn't necessarily a vacation, at least not for me. I was scheduled for final rounds of meetings at PACOM headquarters (Pacific command), the Asia-Pacific Center for Security Studies, the Hawaii Visitors Bureau, and the East-West Center, along with others. Nevertheless, when we landed, I took Catherine's hand and thanked her again. "Aloha, Mr. Ambassador," she smiled back at me.

My meetings at PACOM, particularly with the CINCPAC (Commander-in Chief, Pacific) Admiral Dennis Blair were most significant and relevant to my posting. Denny gave me a comprehensive overview of the strategic importance of the region and our critical alliances there. In particular, he highlighted the ongoing collaboration between the U.S. Navy and the Fijian navy and the strategic value of that relationship. Denny was a fellow Rhodes scholar at Oxford with Bill Clinton and would be the first Director of National Intelligence under President Barack Obama. Denny and I would work closely during my term as ambassador and he and his wife, Dianne, are close friends with Catherine and me to this day.

With my background in tourism and the importance the industry played in the economic and social makeup of the countries I was about to serve, I really wanted to discuss Hawaii's tourism industry and its socio-economic impact on the state. DOS set up a meeting at the governor's office with an assistant who was in charge of the tourism portfolio. The young man was very knowledgeable and in a two-hour meeting, he thoroughly briefed me in all aspects of Hawaii's tourism sector, covering all of the underlying prospects and challenges. Then he handed me some important documents and publications for later reading.

I thanked the young man for his time and courtesies and gave him my calling card as I said goodbye. At that moment, his demeanor and expression changed and he seemed to be gasping for words. "Is there something the matter?" I said. Apologetically, he said that all the time we were meeting, he thought he was briefing the Fijian Ambassador to the U.S.! It never occurred to him that I was the U.S. Ambassador to Fiji. I'm sure the mistake was made because of my ethnic appearance, but I knew it was best to leave that unsaid. His embarrassment was obvious and heartfelt. I told him not to worry as all the information he gave me was still relevant. Then I thanked him profusely and told him what a wonderful job he did and wished him all the best.

Our flight from Honolulu to Fiji on Air New Zealand took us via Auckland and arrived at Nadi airport in the very early hours of the morning. Next would be a short commuter flight to Suva, our destination. We were tired, jet-lagged, and groggy and were met with an equally sleepy protocol officer from the Fiji foreign office. Happily, we settled into the airport VIP lounge where the children immediately slumped into the sofas. I refreshed a bit and got some coffee. Turning, I saw a tall, robust, smart-looking Fijian gentleman walking toward with me with a big smile and outstretched arms.

"Good morning, Mr. Ambassador," he called out. "Bula! Welcome to Fiji! I'm Frank Bainimarama. You can call me Frank." I knew the name. Bainimarama was the chief of the Fijian military and commander of their navy, the first high-ranking Fijian official I was to meet. He was on his way to Singapore for a conference. What a coincidence to be meeting at Nadi airport. Serendipity? Or was it? I'll never know. Frank Bainimarama has been the central and most important figure in the political life of Fiji since that time. Currently, he's the prime minister, serving his second term. Every bit of history that island nation made in the past twenty years bears the mark and stamp of Frank and his policies. All during my stay in Suva, I would have a very cordial and close relationship with him, which I still maintain.

Meeting Frank was just the beginning. Catherine and the children and I were in for quite an adventure. At the time, rousting myself out of my jetlag with the coffee, all I knew for sure was that my ambassadorship was going to be a life experience like no other.

CHAPTER TEN

Ambassador

EMBASSY SUVA WAS A REGIONAL embassy covering four countries—Fiji, Tonga, Tuvalu, and Nauru; and three French departments—Tahiti, New Caledonia, and Wallis and Futuna. All told, the district covered some twelve-million square miles, supposedly the largest in the Department of State, though ninety-eight percent of it was Pacific Ocean.

I had done my homework. I knew the geography and history of these islands. I knew that the Republic of Fiji was an archipelago of more than 330 islands, a third of them permanently inhabited. The two biggest islands, Vitu Levu, where Embassy Suva is located, and Vanua Levu, hold about eighty-five percent of the total population of about a million people. Fiji, with mineral resources, as well as resources from its forests and, of course, the surrounding sea, has a relatively well-developed economy. There is sugar, too, and, naturally, tourism plays a big role. The University of South Pacific is centered in Fiji as is the South Pacific Forum. Fiji is consistently a significant contributor to U.N. peacekeeping forces and the United States has provided its armed services with training.

It was the Dutch, in the mid-seventeenth century, who first explored Fiji. American whaling ships came across Fiji and the other islands of this part of the South Pacific in the early nineteenth century and soon came the inevitable merchant ships and missionary expeditions. The first officially sanctioned U.S. exploration of the area was the Wilkes Expedition, which visited Fiji in the 1840s, but by 1874, Fiji was part of the British Empire and the cultural formation of modern Fiji began. Fiji would remain under British authority until 1970 when it received its independence.

Most of the ethnic Fijians are Melanesian, having settled the islands from Papua New Guinea over three thousand years ago. Over time, Polynesian people and culture began to mix as a result of trade and wars. Then, in its time as a British colony, Fiji adopted many British traits and customs, including a parliamentary and judicial system. But today's biggest holdover from the colonial days is the Indian population. Great Britain imported indentured laborers from India to work the huge sugar cane plantations. Between the 1880s and the early twentieth century, more than 60,000 Indian farmers were brought to Fiji. The Indians were splintered among themselves—most were Hindus, around ten percent were Muslims, and they came from all over India representing different castes and even speaking different languages—but they quickly realized the importance of organizing themselves to defend their rights. When Fiji became independent, the native Fijians were comparatively naïve to the realities of the modern world and unprepared to deal with the better-educated and better-informed Indo-Fijians. Making matters more volatile was that, by then, the Indo-Fijian population had surpassed the ethnic-Fijian population, creating both a social and political imbalance. (Today, because of a significant degree of migration, the ethnic-Fijians are once again the majority.)

It didn't help that there had only ever been minimal interaction between the Indo-Fijians and the ethnic-Fijians. No attempt made to learn each other's language, religion, or culture. Indo-Fijians spoke Hindi, ate their distinctive cuisine, and wore their traditional dresses. Indian women wore their colorful sarees while the Fijian ladies wore their native long dresses. Sulu, the Fijian formal skirt-like outfit worn by all men, was shunned by the Indians even among their high-ranking government officials and other dignitaries. Fijians played rugby; Indians preferred soccer and cricket. Indian music was played on the radio and Indian movies were shown on television and in movie theaters. Fijians were deeply Christian (those early missionary expeditions had been largely successful) while the Indians were mostly either Hindu or Muslim. Most Indians were vegetarians while the Fijians were descendants of vociferous cannibals. In my time there, I hardly saw any intermarriages between the two groups. After a hundred years of living together, the divide between the Indo-Fijians and the ethnic-Fijians couldn't be any starker. Adding to the mix was a population of Europeans and Asians that made up about five percent of Fiji's total populace.

Upon its independence in 1970, a constitution was drawn up that provided fairness for all sides. Ethnic-Fijians and Indo-Fijians were represented equally in the House of Representatives with twenty-two seats each. Then, an additional eight seats were filled by Europeans and other minorities. The head of the government was the prime minister and the ceremonial head of state would be the governor-general, appointed by the British monarchy.

This arrangement kept the peace for a while, until a young army officer named Sitiveni "Steve" Rabuka led a successful coup in 1987, firmly establishing a staunchly nationalistic military dictatorship. Rabuka was a hero to most ethnic- Fijians but was condemned internationally. Fiji was suspended from the British Commonwealth while the governments of Australia and New Zealand imposed stiff economic sanctions. India, however, was notably passive in its reactions.

Rabuka was smart enough to see the writing on the wall and realized he had to change course if Fiji was to prosper and move forward. On this matter, my predecessor, Ambassador Don Gevirtz played a very important role. He told me how he brought Rabuka and moderate Indo-Fijian leaders to sit together and work out a new power-sharing platform under a new constitution. One of the leaders from the Indo-Fijian side was an academic named J. Ram Reddy and Ambassador Gevirtz told me that the first meeting between Rabuka and Reddy took place at the ambassador's residence under the cloak of extreme secrecy. Later, when I met Reddy, he confirmed the details of those meetings and spoke of their intensity. Under the proposed new constitution, the leader with the most seats in the parliament would be prime minister and the cabinet ministers would be appointed proportionately to any party winning at least ten percent of the vote. Maybe not the best solution, but perhaps a step in the right direction. Fiji became a republic.

It was in 1999, as my nomination process was going through its hurdles in Washington D.C., that Fiji's first election under the new constitution took place. It was a huge surprise. Both Rabuka and Reddy were thoroughly trounced, repudiated by the people. Both their parties overwhelmingly lost out in the electoral contest. Mahendra Chaudhry and his Fiji Labor Party won the majority of seats in the parliament. Chaudhry was a talented and charismatic union leader, but also a polarizing personality. He complained of disparity and injustices meted out to the Indo-Fijian community by past governments and sought to rectify them. Although he followed the constitution in appointing opposition party ministers, which made most of his cabinet Fijian, he still could not appease the ethnic Fijian sentiments. He and his government were deeply suspect in Fijian nationalist circles and in the military.

It was in the midst of this set of circumstances that my family and I landed in Suva. I was excited to be there, of course, but in the back of my mind was an uneasy feeling. Here I was, the first Asian-American-Muslim Chief of Mission, placed into a racially polarized country simmering with internecine rift and mistrust.

But first things first. My immediate project had to do with the ambassador's residence. It wasn't big enough to accommodate the size of my family! Fortunately, the Department of State agreed to extend one of the wings, adding a bedroom and a recreation space. Today, the residence stands a little more imposing, a small legacy that I trust the ambassadors who have followed me have appreciated.

As ambassador, my first official order of business was to present my credentials to the President of the Republic of Fiji, Ratu Sir Kamisese Mara. Presenting one's credentials is always the first responsibility for any ambassador. As the Paramount Chief of the Lau Islands of Eastern Fiji, President Mara had led his people to independence from Britain, becoming Fiji's first prime minister in 1970. He had retired in 1987, before the coup, but then came back onto the scene afterward and was now the ceremonial president, the position in the pre-republic days that had been referred to as governor-general.

On September 13, 1999, I was driven to the Government House (as they still called the president's residence per British tradition) in the presidential limo. My deputy chief of mission, Ron McMullen, followed behind. The motorcade wound along palm-lined Queen Elizabeth drive, hugging the shoreline of the Pacific Ocean, to the impressive presidential compound. The Government House was a stately Georgian mansion built in 1928 to serve as the residence of the colonial governor. It rested on acres of undulating green land, with palm trees, bougainvillea, and all manner of exotic tropical flowers. After independence from British rule, the Government House had become the official residence of the governor-general. When Fiji became a republic in 1987, it became the president's residence.

The motorcade pulled in and I was welcomed warmly with a salute by the colorful contingent of the presidential guards dressed in their traditional uniform. Then I was escorted by the chief of protocol up the red-carpeted steps from the car portico, into the white mansion, and to the president's chamber. President Mara was six-foot, five-inches with a towering personality and an imperial presence to match. He greeted me most graciously.

The credential ceremony was relatively simple, after which President Mara walked me to the main grand room where we sat down for tea. After exchanging a few pleasantries, he asked, "When are you bringing back the Peace Corps?" Indeed, the Peace Corps had been withdrawn in the aftermath of the 1987 coup, though it still had a robust presence in Tonga and a small one in Tuvalu. No doubt the work of the Peace Corps in Fiji had had a great impact. I assured him that as Fiji was making a successful transition to democratic governance, I would work very hard to bring the Peace Corps back. He smiled broadly at my answer. Of course, how could I have known then that my work in this regard would ultimately be interrupted by uncontrollable circumstances?

As per diplomatic traditions and niceties, President Mara conveyed his best wishes and warm regards for President Clinton and his family, then walked me down to the portico from where I was to depart. As I walked back down the red-carpeted steps, I noticed the presidential limo was gone. The official ambassador car was still there, but with a noticeable difference. The left-side fender was now adorned with the stars and stripes, and the right with the ambassadorial standard. The meaning of the flags was clear. No longer was I ambassador-designate. I was now *ambassador*. I slid into the back seat and we drove off, my emotions flying every bit as grand as the flags fluttering off the hood of the car.

I thought of my father at that moment and how he had flown the Pakistani flag. Now I was flying the American flag and it made me proud. Later, after my ambassador service, my brother

Farruk would retire from his position with the World Bank and become education minister of Bangladesh. Farruk would fly the Bangladeshi flag. One family, three flags. I wonder to this day how many other families in the world can boast such a thing? Not many. Perhaps no one before us has ever done so.

The ride back from the president's house to the embassy on Loftus Street took about twenty minutes and in those twenty minutes, the prior twenty years flashed before me. I thought of all that had happened to get me where I now was. I remembered Bob Nash telling me the president had wanted an administration that reflected a cross-section of real Americans. The president had said as much in his second inaugural speech. I was now a part of that administration; I was a part of that cross-section. I thought of getting my citizenship, the oath-taking, my first meeting with President Clinton, my swearing-in ceremony. It all passed through my mind at once and it felt to me as if the car was gliding above the ground as it swept along the edge of the Pacific Ocean.

Finally, the car came to a stop at the chancery. I quickly alighted and went straight to my top-floor office. Out of the window, I could see the Fiji sun shining brightly over the sprawling ocean. But the responsibilities of the office left me no further time for reflections that day. There were a thousand details that needed tending to. In fact, the following week was extremely hectic. I had to get caught up with different aspects of the mission—there were personnel issues, team meetings, bilateral affairs, and more. In between, I had to make the obligatory rounds of courtesy calls to different ministers, the speaker of the parliament, the leader of the opposition, fellow ambassadorial colleagues, and others. The invitations for receptions, dinners, and speaking engagements began piling up immediately. I was on overdrive, trying to learn the many nuances of my new responsibilities.

Fortunately, I had the support of a very capable and qualified deputy chief of mission in Ron McMullen, who would later become ambassador to Eritrea. Ron had come to serve with me after holding similar positions at other embassies, and was a straightforward, no-nonsense professional with strong Iowan values. I made clear to him that my modus operandi was to rely on him as my chief operating officer, to make sure "the trains run on time," responsible for all day-to-day activities. My style, learned in business, was to empower people around me. I saw my role as akin to a chief executive officer, responsible for executing the overall mandate of the mission, including the expansion of bilateral relationships and the conducting of diplomacy at the highest level. Having people like Ron helped that mission succeed.

Despite the whirlwind pace, I was feeling grounded and beginning to get acclimated as ambassador. Quickly, things seemed to fall into place. An order to everything materialized. All was well. Until, that is, I came home to our residence one evening to see all four of my children distraught, eyes red with tears. The issue? School uniforms. Although the kids were enrolled in the International School in Suva, the required uniform was the traditional Fijian sulu, the skirt-like wraparound worn by both boys and girls. The children did not react well. All of them were ready to pack and leave for home without any further notice or delay. I was at a loss but assured them that I would investigate the matter. The next morning, I called the school principal, Peter Kristolites, and headed straight to see him. When I explained my grave domestic predicament, Peter was most gracious and understanding. He said he would make an exception for my children and they could attend school in their respective shorts or jeans. Peace at home was restored. One week later, I came home to find the kids all wearing sulus. "We felt awkward with everyone else wearing them," they said. "And besides, in this hot weather, they're actually okay."

And thus the quandary of the sulus, the first major crisis of my ambassadorship, came to a peaceful and agreeable resolution for all concerned.

*My father, M. Osman Ghani, as a PhD student
at the University of London, 1935-1937.*

My mother, Shamsun Nahar. Simple, elegant, loving.

Catherine's father, Marine Corporal George Pennacchi,
World War II, all of seventeen years old.

High school picture of Sally Lozito, Catherine's mother.

Me at Saint Mary's School, 1959.

Catherine's high school picture.

Happy Hoosier! Indiana University, Bloomington, 1973.

One of my very favorite pictures of Catherine and Me.
Mid-1980s. So many magical moments ahead of us.

October 26, 1992 Four Dollars

Forbes

Even the most crowded and competitive businesses offer opportunities to those who can develop some kind of an edge. In a service business, Osman Siddique figured out how to give extra service at no extra cost.

In the shadow of American Express

Travelogue's Osman Siddique **Painstakingly building a $40 million business offering extra service to demanding travelers.**

By Tatiana Pouschine

THERE ARE only 32 travel agencies in the country that generate more than $100 million in revenues. Big corporate business tends to go to travel industry giants like American Express, Carlson Travel, Thomas Cook, Rosenbluth and U.S. Travel

I enjoyed much favorable press during my successful time in business.

*With President George H. W. Bush in the
Oval Office of the White House, 1992.*

*With Senator Ted Kennedy, 1994 fundraiser
at his home in McLean, Virginia.*

November 17, 1994

Mr. and Mrs. Osman Siddique
c/o Travelogue, Inc.
1201 New York Avenue, NW
Suite 280
Washington, DC 20005

Dear Osman and Catherine:

Now that I have a moment to relax, I want to thank you, most warmly and sincerely, for all of your wonderful help throughout my campaign for re-election to the Senate. I couldn't have done it without you. And the loss of so many Democrats in other races makes your support more vital than ever.

I look forward to the coming battles in the Senate and the country with renewed commitment to fight for the values and causes that you and I care so much about. It was an honor to stand with you in this campaign, and it will be an honor to stand with you in facing the challenges ahead.

Most importantly of all, Vicki and I are grateful for your friendship. You were always there to lend a hand, and we can't thank you enough for all that you did. Your support and loyalty mean the world to us, and we send our heartfelt thanks and best wishes for the holidays.

As ever,

Ted

many thanks.

Senator Kennedy was always generous with his gratitude.

With my friend and well-wisher, Hillary Clinton.

*With Catherine and the president at the
White House Christmas party, 1996.*

INDIANA UNIVERSITY

January 13, 2000

OFFICE OF THE
UNIVERSITY
CHANCELLOR

The Honorable M. Osman Siddique
Ambassador of the Untied States
U.S. Embassy
P.O. Box 218
Suva
FIJI ISLANDS

Dear Osman:

     I appreciate your good letter of December 16 and the details about your appointment as Ambassador. Again, my hearty congratulations.

     I'm delighted that your education here prepared you for such an illustrious career. I hope you find your appointment extremely rewarding; I know you will be a credit to both our country and the university.

     With warm good wishes,

          Cordially,

          Herman B Wells
          University Chancellor

HBW:lb

Owen Hall 100
Bloomington, Indiana
47405-5200

812-855-6647
Fax: 812-855-5642

This letter of support from Herman B Wells
of my alma mater meant the world to me.

Prime Minister Frank Bainimarama,
the first Fijian official to greet me with, "Bula!"

Me with the president of the Republic of Fiji, Ratu Sir
Kamisese Mara, after my credential presentation. Standing
behind me is my Deputy Chief of Mission Ron McMullen.

With His Majesty Taufa'ahau Tupou IV, King of Tonga at my credential-presentation ceremony, all of us in our formal best.

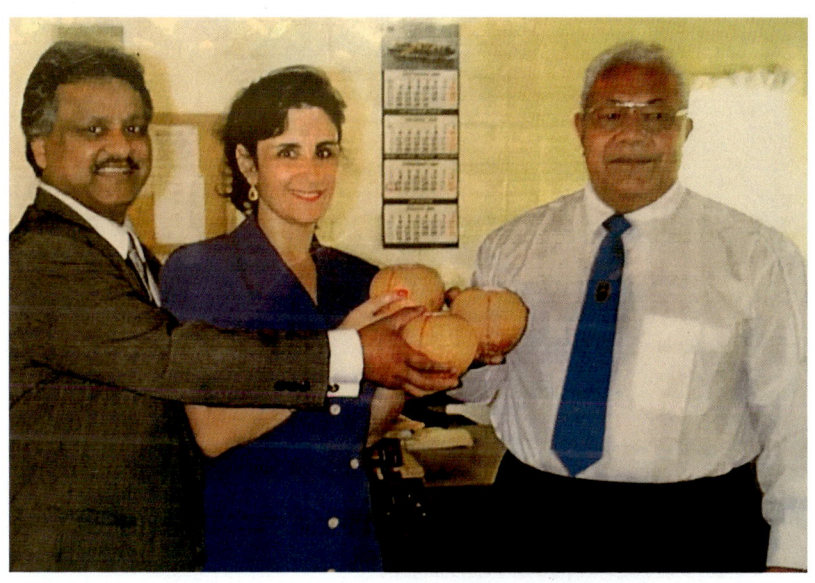

Catherine and me with Governor-General Sir Tomasi Puapua of Tuvalu, toasting with coconuts at my credential-presentation ceremony.

With Prime Minister Mahendra Chaudhry of
Fiji at the ambassador residence.

At the SANGAM ceremony in Suva,
being welcomed in the ritualistic Hindu tradition.

Celebrating President Mara's eightieth birthday at his Lau Island home.

High Chief "Ratu Zack" with an embassy guard at the residence.

US Ambassador Osman Siddique

New office for Habitat

By REJINAL DUTT

US Ambassador Osman Siddique was the chief guest at the opening of an office for Habitat for ...

houses in more than 60 countries worldwide.

It began its operations in Fiji in 1993, buildin...

US data processing plant set up in Fiji

By Ranadi Johnston

Data processing using satellite technology could reap up to $1 billion for Fiji.

That's the prediction made by the United States of America's new ambassador to Fiji, Osman Siddique.

Speaking to The Sun, he reveals that this will soon be a reality here with the set up of such a company in Nadi.

"The final negotiation has taken place and infrastructure development is going on at a very slow," Siddique says of the deal with the American company.

However, no names will be released at this stage.

Siddique did hint at the type of industry the company would be servicing.

"Airlines - for example - have thousands and thousands of airline tickets to process.

"In America, labour is expensive - so most of the data entry is done in Barbados," he says.

"Fiji has the advantage of being more than 12 hours ahead of the US. That's not the only attraction.

"According to Siddique, the fact that Fiji is an English-speaking country, with fairly developed communications services helps in its case.

"This and a stable base of well educated people," he puts in.

"... India, Malaysia and ...

Singapore will be Fiji's main competitors in the data processing industry.

But says Siddique: "There are good set-up for Fiji would be an attractive alternative."

Employment creation is on top of the list of the benefits that would arise from such a venture.

Other flow-on effects would be an increase in consumer spending, sale of real estate property, education levels, more skilled workers, more white collar jobs and ultimately, more tax revenue for the government.

Some 200 jobs are likely to be created, some for overseas managers and trainers.

Commenting on the feasibility of the data processing industry here, the new ambassador says that the current low labour cost and Fiji time difference with the US would be the major factor in its success.

In late 1992, there were talks of Qantas shifting its data processing and ticketing office here but after strong protests from its Australian employees, the project was shelved.

Besides data processing, other US companies have also expressed interest in ventures as tourists and the timber industry. This includes Kentucky Fried Chicken, the famous restaurant chain.

Siddique ... interest from US investors

ALL ethnic groups should be encouraged to have faith that they can succeed in commerce.

Addressing the Fiji-US Business Council on Thursday, United States ambassador to Fiji Osman Siddique said that in Fiji the Indo-Fijian business men and women should teach and be mentors to indigenous Fijian.

"Clearly all people of Fiji can prosper from business.

"Some of the largest firms in the world were started by one enterprising person with a vision and access to enough capital to realise that vision," he said.

The ambassador referred to Microsoft former boss, Bill Gates, to put his point across.

COMMANDANT EN CHEF DES FORCES AMÉRICA... L'OCÉAN INDIEN

...miral Dennis C. Blair reçu à Tahiti

...Dennis C. Blair, commandant en chef ...es américaines dans le Pacifique ...l'océan Indien effectue une visite ...x jours en Polynésie française.

...e amiral Amaury du ...commandant supérieur ...es armées en Polynésie ...a reçu hier au Taaone le ...dant de plus de la moitié ...es militaires des Etats-...n effet l'amiral Dennis

C.Blair depuis son quartier général à Hawaii a la charge de toutes les forces américaines déployées dans le Pacifique et l'océan Indien.

Les honneurs ont été rendus à la délégation dès son arrivée au

Les honneurs ont été rendus, hier au Taaone, au commandant e... chef des forces américaines dans le Pacifique et l'océan Indien... l'amiral Dennis C. Blair.

Taaone. Le chef des armées américaines du Pacifique était en effet accompagné par une quinzaine de personnes dont les ambassadeurs Twining, conseiller politique de l'amiral et Siddique, ambassadeur des Fidji.

L'amiral du Chéné devait discuter avec son homologue des ...

marine américaine dans l... Pacifique, en Nouvelle-Zéland... lors de la réunion des forces d... Pacifique, il y a deux semaines.

Au cours de ce bref séjour... Tahiti, l'amiral américain a re... contré le haut-commissaire Je... Aribaud, et le vice-président ... gouvernement, Édouard Fritch. ... délégation visite... matin ... de répartir ...

Americans like

VASEMACA RARABICI

FIJI will benefit from American assistance as it has a lot of potential to develop in various areas of investment.

These were the words of new American Ambassador Osman Siddique in Suva yesterday.

Mr Siddique who arrived into the country earlier this month, officially took up his post as ambassador, after presenting his credentials to the President, Ratu Sir Kamisese Mara, at Government House yesterday.

He said the United States is willing to fund projects which are worthwhile and looks forward to working with Fiji in all fields of investment.

Mr Siddique is currently the President and Chief Executive Officer of ITI/Travelogue, a corporate travel management company he founded in 1976.

He has received several awards for his fast-growing business and has been prominently profiled in international ...

US Ambassador says tourism world's largest industry

By HARI GAUNDER

TOURISM is America's leading export earner, creating a trade surplus of nearly US$19 billion and injecting $95 billion (Fijian $190 billion) into the US economy, says American Ambassador, Osman Siddique.

Mr Siddique made the comment at the Pacific Asia Travel Association meeting at the Tanoa International Hotel in Nadi yesterday.

He said a record 46.5 million international travellers visited America in 1999.

"More than a million people work in jobs supported by the spending of international visitors," he said.

"This is good since 95 percent of the businesses, which are small and medium sized, enterprises, which are the back bone of our economy."

He said that tourism in the US is expected to stage a strong

showing by 2002, with arrivals topping 52 million and expenditures expected to exceed $US110 (FJ220) billion.

Mr Siddique said that according to the World Trade Organisation's (WTO) conference last year, "travel and tourism is the world's largest industry."

"Global tourism shows consistent year on year growth with 43 percent per annum between 1989 and 1998," he revealed.

"In 1999, an estimated 65 million people spent approximately $US455 billion or roughly $920 billion Fijian dollars o travel."

According to research unde taken by WTO, this growth trer will continue, he added

Said Siddique: "Actual WTO is forecasting a 200 pe cent increase in internation tourist arrivals between yea 2000 and 2020."

THE FIJI SUN - SATU

---

ntrywide

nternet o close ich, poor lisparity

OUNTRIES like Fiji will unable to compete with a fast moving infor tion driven global village less education is widely seminated to the general pulace, said American mbassador Osman iddique.

Mr Siddique said the answer in technology network schoo cities ing play rich tw velc and cou roc

Mr Siddique asked the students whether they thought it interesting that the biggest problems in the country and throughout the world relate not to some modern problem but they are rooted in the oldest, most primitive problem of human societies.

"We are still afraid of people who are different people who look different

Culture of free trade

Envoy promotes ethnic involvement

By PAUL YAVALA

OSMAN SIDDIQUE, the US ambassador to Fiji, believes more can and should be done to encourage entrepreneurship, privatisation and free trade in Fiji.

Mr Siddique made the call while addressing a meeting of the Fiji-US Business Council in Suva.

He said there were courses on entrepreneurship in business schools all over America as well as at the University of the South Pacific.

"But there needs to be more incentives and rewards for entrepreneurial achievement," Mr Siddique told the council.

"You, as successful businessmen and women, know that recognition and incentives help to build a better and more productive workforce."

Calling for a change in attitude, Mr Siddique said Fiji needed to foster and develop a culture of entrepreneurship among the ethnic Fijian community.

He said all ethnic groups should be encouraged to have faith that they can succeed in commerce.

"In this respect, particularly the Indo-businessmen and women, need to do a little more mentoring and catering to their ethnic brothers and sisters," said Mr Siddique who is a successful businessman in his own right in the United States.

On privatisation, Mr Siddique said Fiji had made a good start in attracting investment.

But, he said, still more could be done in privatising certain government activities.

"There is clearly a role for government in establishing the basis for a sound and sustainable economy, but I have always found that businessmen are better than

moving to privatise government holdings.

Mr Siddique said the Government's role was to establish a working environment that would allow these enterprises to flourish and to provide and enforce a regulatory framework.

This reduced distortions and allowed decisions, including wage rates, to be driven by market forces.

Privatisation, Mr Siddique added, would bring some much needed foreign investment and allow the latest in technology to transfer into Fiji.

On free trade Mr Sid

producers is understandable, but at what price?" said Mr Siddique.

"All the families in Fiji pay the price, not only in higher costs but also in lack of variety, smaller supply and often, narrow range of quality."

Mr Siddique said Fiji should compete with its strengths and use its advantages.

These included:
■ A large workforce;
■ Competitive wage rates;
■ Natural land and sea resources; and
■ Location between major markets of

The Fiji-US Business Council now has more than 30 members and Mr Siddique has urged more Fiji businesses to join the council and take advantage of the growth in the US economy.

He said trade had helped fuel the current boom in the US economy.

Measured in terms of their purchasing power, incomes in the US were 27 per cent higher than its counterparts in Japan and 41 per cent higher than in Germany.

Osman Siddique — "there needs to be more incentives for entrepreneurial achievements"

---

iness here

---

e Minister in this calls for a sustain rate of six per his budgetary can only be at ugh enhanced nvestment," he

e said the global would expand ased trade and eer flow of capi interest of Fiji ions.

ble, the global be built on a political foun-

e supported by of community, an appreciation non humanity of the world

---

The press treated me well in Fiji and covered quite a bit of our activities.

I always appreciated the chance to participate in the colorful customs and celebrations of the island nations of my consular district.

THE WHITE HOUSE

WASHINGTON

May 9, 2000

The Honorable M. Osman Siddique
American Ambassador
Suva

Dear Osman:

    Happy 50th Birthday! Hillary and
I send our very best wishes for health
and happiness in the coming year.

Sincerely,

Bill Clinton

Birthday greetings from the president.

During the coup, I was inspired and encouraged by many letters of support like this one from an anonymous Fijian. The note reads:

Dear Mr. Siddique,

You have been a fantastically good ambassador and we appreciate what you have done post May 19, 2000. We—the victims of the coup—are sustained by your courage and steadfast commitment to the universal principles, values, and ideals of sound democratic governance. You did not succumb to the bogus Pacific Way of resolving the crisis as a way that purports to be superior to the UN Charter. Thank you.

Regards and best wishes to your family.

—Da Silent Majority

A recent picture with the boss.

What I'm most proud of by far—my family. From left to right:
Zachary, Leila, Omar, Catherine, Julene, me, and son-in-law Euan.

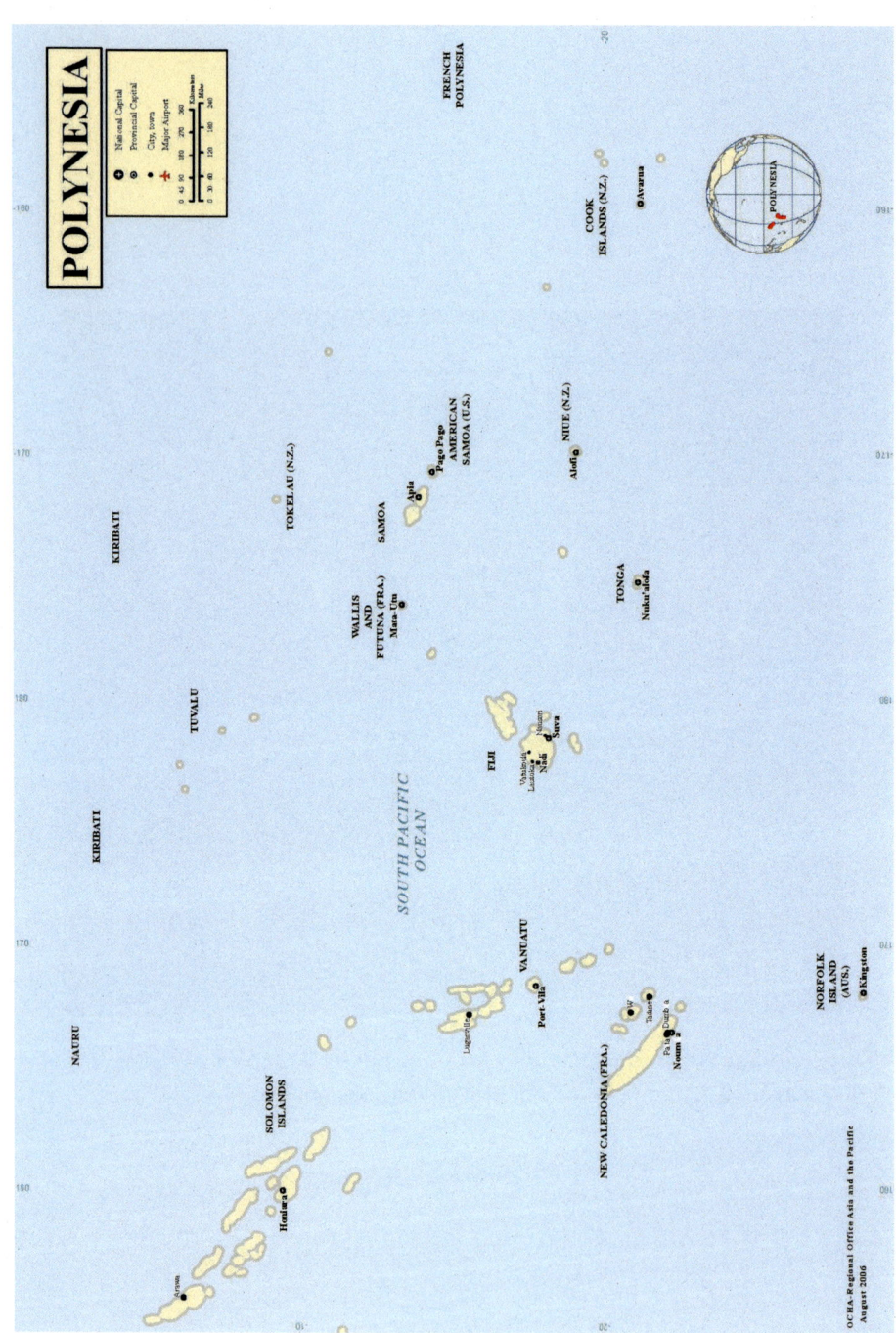

Oceania

CHAPTER ELEVEN

Oceania

A LITTLE MORE THAN A week after I presented my credentials in Fiji, I was off, with my family, to present my credentials in Tonga. The Kingdom of Tonga is a Polynesian archipelago comprised of more than 170 islands with a surface area of 290 square miles. Thirty-six of the islands are inhabited, with Tongatapu being the main island where some seventy percent of the kingdom's 200,000 people make their home. This island is protected by lagoons and limestones and we found ourselves fascinated by a natural water show of extraordinary blowholes.

Reliable sources told me that more Tongans lived overseas than in Tonga itself, most of them in Australia, New Zealand, and the United States. Repatriation of money by these overseas Tongans provided a big boost to the country's economy, helping to lift the standards of many. Two important crops, vanilla and a special variety of melon, the latter shipped almost exclusively to Japan, provided a living for many local farmers.

Tonga was one of the Pacific's established Polynesian monarchies when the Europeans arrived in force in the late eighteenth century. With the help of missionaries, Tonga declared itself to be a European-style constitutional monarchy in 1875. In reality, however, the monarchy had total power. Tonga had a parliament, but with two-thirds of its members appointed by the king or by the country's nobles, and only one-third by the commoners, the real power was wielded from the palace. This pretense of democracy was still the situation when I arrived. There was an underlying dissatisfaction among the general population and some talk of impending liberalization, but nothing would be changed during my term there and little remains changed to this day.

The capital and largest city is Nuki'alofa, and as we drove its roads, I was surprised to see many homes looking more like what you might see in an American suburb, rather than a Polynesian island. I noticed a lot of big American cars, too. For the presentation of credentials, the king, His Majesty Taufa'ahau Tupou IV, required formal attire, and not just a nice suit or even a tuxedo. Formal attire for the king meant morning coat with tails, top hat, and white gloves. I rented an outfit suitable for the occasion from New Zealand and had it shipped in. Catherine had to wear a long dress, long white gloves up to her elbow, and a hat. The children were dressed appropriately as well. I imagined the king had wanted to emulate the formal traditions of the British monarchy. There was a major difference, however, between royal ceremonies in Great Britain and royal ceremonies in Tonga: in Tonga it was 105 degrees Fahrenheit. In the shade!

On the morning of the ceremony, September 22, 1999, sweltering in our formal best, we waited for the motorcade from the palace to pick us up at our lodgings. But when it arrived, a problem arose. The Tongan protocol officer advised us that, per tradition, only the ambassador and his wife were invited to the credential presentation ceremony; children were not allowed. This was contrary to what had been previously arranged. When I looked at the faces of the kids, it didn't take me more than a second to make up my mind. I politely told the protocol officer that if that was the case, we would be flying back to Fiji that morning and would very much look forward to the re-scheduling of the ceremony to another date, confident, I told him, that the rescheduled ceremony would be one in which my children would be welcomed. The nervous protocol officer excused himself, made a few frantic phone calls, probably to the foreign office and the palace, and came back to tell me that, as a matter of fact, it had been decided that my family could join me that morning, after all.

King Tupou IV, ruler of Tonga since 1965, was a heavy-set man in his early eighties. At one point, he drew global attention as the world's heaviest monarch, weighing in at over 465 pounds. His official limousine was nothing less than a Winnebago RV. As it turns out, Tongans are among the heaviest people in the world. King Tupou IV at least had the good sense to lead a campaign against obesity. When I met him, I was told that he was on a diet and had lost almost 200 pounds from his peak weight. But he still relished one of his favorite meals, a dish made with meat from bats. The king received my family and me very cordially and seemed at ease with my children. I was presented with a quite impressive honor guard ceremony and the band played the Tongan and American national anthems with due solemnity. I noticed the king lip-synching "The Star-Spangled Banner" in its entirety and he seemed very proud of it.

In my time as ambassador, I would come to see that the king was respected and obeyed by Tongans, but perhaps not revered. Despite his good intentions, he did not seem to manage the economy very well, and he allowed some misappropriation of the country's scarce resources to the detriment of the treasury. Most troubling was the blatant corruption within the royal family. The crown prince and crown princess treated the Tongan treasury as their own little piggy bank and had no reservations about reaching into it for their own personal use. I was told that, at a huge premium to her, the princess had forced the king to break off a long-standing relationship with Taiwan and recognize Beijing. Subsequently, the palace pushed the Chinese to move into the sprawling empty Taiwanese embassy at an exorbitantly high rent. The princess also sold Tonga's satellite space (TongaSat) to the Chinese, keeping for herself the lucrative proceeds.

Despite all this, going back to the Second World War, Tonga had been a good and reliable partner to the U.S. In later years, Tonga would also be a good partner in our war on terror. During my service, I would always be happy to visit our well-managed Peace Corps contingent there. It was based in Tongatapu but spread out over much of the country and worked in education, health care, the nation's fisheries, and in other important sectors. The locals very much appreciated their work. Other commercial interests were limited to small to mid-size businesses. I would be proud to inaugurate an Ace Hardware store in Nuku'iolofe and even to bring an American KFC to the negotiating table with a local partner. In the time I spent in Tonga, however, I would be disappointed to never have the time to visit the beautiful whale watching island of Vava'u, a popular destination for yachts and sailing boats from all over the world. One can't see and do everything.

A month after presenting my credentials in Tonga, I traveled to Nauru to present my credentials there. The Republic of Nauru, formerly known as Pleasant Island, is only about eight square miles with a population of around 11,000. It's the third smallest nation by area in the world behind Vatican City and Monaco. From our descending airplane, Nauru looked to me like a doughnut with the middle gnawed out. As a result of years of extraction of phosphate, used in fertilizer, the interior appeared like some alien planet.

One of the main sources of phosphate is guano. Bird droppings! It seems that for thousands of years, Nauru must have been a stopping off place for the many seabirds of the South Pacific. The island's phosphate was discovered by the Germans in the late 1800s and Nauru became a German colony not long afterward. It remained one until the end of World War I when it became a territory of the League of Nations, but more or less under Australian control. The Japanese occupied the island during the Second World War, and after Japan's defeat, control of the island fell into the hands of the United Nations. Finally, in 1968, Nauru became its own country.

Phosphate made the new country wealthy, but the government mismanaged the island's money. Nauruan leaders lived in posh luxury hotels and invested the country's wealth as if it was their own in real estate abroad. They even invested in Broadway plays and a French opera! Meanwhile, the country itself teetered on bankruptcy. Worse, the mining rendered the interior of the island unlivable. There was virtually no agriculture and Nauru became dependent on imported food, most of it canned and processed. Before long, Nauru's population earned the unfortunate distinction of being the most obese people in the world, more so than even the Tongans. Cases of diabetes skyrocketed.

We flew into the single-runway airport in the district of Yaren. Although Nauru had no official capital, Yaren was where parliament and the government offices were located. On October 19, 1999, I presented my credentials to President Rene Harris whom I found to be a very gracious gentleman. He greeted me with a guard of honor and later hosted a grand banquet dinner. As it happens, he had just returned from the U.S., having attended the United Nations General Assembly sessions in New York. He told me that he had been overwhelmingly impressed by the protection he'd been given by our secret service during his visit. He elaborated in minute detail the scope of their efforts. He'd been received immediately from his airplane, he'd been whisked through customs, and he'd been provided with a motorcade that drove him to and from the airport with sirens wailing. Not only that, everywhere he went, including to the restroom, he'd had a security detail escorting him. I told him that's the way we treat every head of state, whether you're the president of China or the president of Nauru. "When it comes to protection," I told him, "to us, size does not matter!"

Humor and niceties aside, however, I had two compelling matters to discuss with President Harris. First was the issue of shell-banking and second was the sale of passports. We had intel that billions of dollars were being laundered, especially by the Russians, through fake bank accounts established in Nauru. Meanwhile, the sale of bogus passports was creating potential national security issues for everybody, including the U.S. When I mentioned these two matters to President Harris, he feigned ignorance or inattention. I pressed on, at one point remarking that these dual sources of income would never offset the losses his country suffered because of poor investments and corruption. Finally, President Harris agreed to investigate the problems and to cooperate with the U.S. to find a resolution. Subsequently, a team of U.S. government officials, including the FBI, followed up and began an investigation that continued even after I left office.

The final stop on my credential-presenting circuit was Tuvalu. Formerly known as Ellice Island, Tuvalu has a population only slightly higher than Nauru's and is spread out over nine island groups. The capital island of Funafuti encircles a large lagoon. On our first visit there, my wife and I walked around the lagoon—the entire length of Funafuti—in a single afternoon. I cabled the State Department, presenting my impressions from the walk and from my other observations of Funafuti, and the information was distributed throughout the department and even to the U.S. Pacific Command. As it happens, there's a great deal of interest in Tuvalu. With an average elevation of just 6.6 feet above sea level, Tuvalu is a sort of canary in the coal mine when it comes to climate change. The country could be one of the first nations to experience, to a disastrous extent, the effects of sea-level rise as a result of global warming.

Tuvalu was of strategic importance to the U.S. during World War II. The Marines landed on Funafuti in 1942 and built an airstrip, still in use today as the country's only airport. The country is still of strategic importance in that part of the world and a trust fund established by the United Kingdom, New Zealand, and Australia of around $100 million provides much of the government revenue. There are bilateral trade initiatives with other countries, too, plus revenue from fishing licenses and the South Pacific Tuna Treaty, which allows access to U.S. fishing vessels. An astute California entrepreneur leased the country's top-level internet domain (.tv) to sell domains to people who want to set up television-related websites. Overall, the government of Tuvalu has been very prudent in the management of its economy.

Catherine and I arrived on the island of Funafuti on November 29, 1999, in a small Air Fiji plane after an especially rough flight. After being received by Tuvaluan officials from the Ministry of Foreign Affairs, we headed for the only hotel on the island. With very little rest, we found ourselves having to get ready for the credential presentation ceremony. All either one of us wanted to do was take a shower, but we were quickly dismayed to find no running water at the hotel. I called the front desk, which had no explanation for the lack of water, but agreed to send a bucket of water to us. Catherine wasn't particularly happy about the situation, and neither was I, but somehow we managed to clean up before making our way to the modest governor's mansion.

Relating this experience to the Japanese ambassador on my return to Suva, the ambassador mentioned that something very similar had happened to him. The dearth of water was, he told me, quite intentional. The idea was to impress upon visiting ambassadors the urgent need for a desalinization plant, which they hoped we would petition our respective governments for after our uncomfortable experiences.

At any rate, Governor-General Sir Tomasi Puapua was a stocky, mild-mannered gentleman who, at the presentation ceremony, offered us very refreshing coconut water, served in its original casing, to toast with. And thus, I had now presented my credentials to all four island nations.

While I was in Tuvalu, I was invited to visit their only school. The boys and girls put on a local dance and music show in my honor. When the festivities ended, the school authorities approached me with a request: to help build toilets for the kids. When I asked where they were relieving themselves now, their answer was, "By the oceanside and bushes." I knew the money the country had in its treasury and I was appalled by this set of circumstances. It was all I could do to rein in my anger as I responded. "The U.S. government always lends a hand to small nations and their people," I said, "but I will never support your request for school toilets for these kids. I know how much money you have in your trust fund and from other sources. I know you can spend a few thousand dollars to give these kids the basic necessity of working toilets. What else is your money for if not for something as pressing as this? No, I'm sorry your request is unacceptable and, actually, quite preposterous." This left them stunned and more than a little embarrassed. My understanding is that new toilets were built soon after.

Leaving Tuvalu was not easy. Air Fiji had only two flights a week and as a result of various circumstances, our scheduled departure was delayed twice, much to Catherine's chagrin. My wife has always been the adventurous type, fascinated by new culture and old history, ready to explore new places and vistas.

Tuvalu, unfortunately, didn't offer much to keep her interest alive. The food at the hotel was barely adequate, with the same things served at every meal, and there were no restaurants, museums, or shops. She kept it from me but, later, I would overhear her telling a friend that the only time she had cried during our marriage was when our flight out of Tuvalu had been canceled for the second time. I could not blame her in the least.

Finally, we made it back to Fiji. They had welcomed us in Tonga, Nauru, and Tuvalu, three places I could never have imagined I would have seen in my lifetime. Although there were similarities, each was unique, each with its own history and culture, and each with its own challenges, and opportunities. Overall, I was fascinated by what I'd seen and experienced, and as our small plane touched down in Fiji, a single thought occurred to me: it's good to be an ambassador!

CHAPTER TWELVE

Flying the Flag

AFTER ALL THE INTRODUCTIONS AND presentations and for-
malities were out of the way, my work as ambassador began in
earnest. One of the first items on my agenda was to restore our
military training program in Fiji. The International Military
Education and Training (IMET) program, established by
Congress as part of the International Security Assistance and
Arms Export Control Act of 1976, provides defense support for
our friends around the world. Typically, this support takes the
form of training that gives our allies the knowledge they need to
keep their nations secure from threats, both inside and outside.
IMET had been suspended in Fiji after the 1987 coup, but with
the strides the government was taking, we felt it was time to
reinstate it. Speaking to reporters in my first press conference, I

remarked, "The U.S. strongly supports Fiji's democratic stand, and as a tangible sign of that support, the Clinton administration has notified Congress of its intention to resume its training of the Fijian military's peace-keeping ability. Fiji's commitment in this area is world-class and because of that, the U.S. will work to further strengthen its institutional capacity."

Additionally, I continued to work with CINCPAC Admiral Denny Blair who had briefed me so thoroughly on the strategic importance of the area and the vital role of the U.S. Navy's extensive fleet. He and I always made sure that U.S. naval ships were able to transit uninterrupted and anchor along the shores of Suva with unimpeded access to all available facilities for refueling and restocking. We needed to ensure the safety of our sailors who would disembark for shore excursions. State-of-the-art frigates, nuclear-powered submarines, and even aircraft carriers made their way to Suva. Each visit of a major naval ship meant anywhere from $250,000 to $500,000 for the city coffers. Refueling alone could run more than a couple hundred thousand dollars.

One of the major attractions when these ships came ashore was always the Captain's Lunch, which was a customary event. As the personal representative of the commander-in-chief, I was always received onboard with the appropriate protocol and accompanying military honors. I also had the privilege of inviting a few guests. Those invitations were some of the most sought-out invites for the local dignitaries, civic leaders, and my diplomatic colleagues. One person who always appreciated an invitation was Commodore Frank Bainimarama, the head of Fiji military and himself a navy man. He enjoyed the tours of the ship, always conducted personally by a captain who was typically a rear-admiral. The lunches themselves were enjoyable, too, as I found the navy chefs to be quite excellent.

One burgeoning American enterprise in Fiji was Fiji Water and soon after my arrival I became acquainted with the company's founder and chairman David Gilmour and its chief executive Doug Carlson. Fiji Water's supply came from an artesian aquifer on the main island of Viti Levu. Thanks to David's marketing prowess, Fiji Water was having tremendous success in the U.S. and throughout the world and demand for Fiji Water's product was exceeding supply. To expand production, it was necessary to acquire more of the land that held the water underneath, and to improve the infrastructure. Widening old roads, building new ones, constructing additional bridges, and increasing the port facilities were all a necessary part of the company's expansion. But the Fiji government was cool to the demands of Fiji Water, citing budgetary constraints and low incentives for the government exchequer. The bottom line, which quickly became clear to me, was that they wanted more excise taxes.

At a meeting with the prime minister, I carried a bottle of Fiji Water in my hand and told him that Fiji Water was making a positive impact on the image of his country. It was the water of choice for celebrities, athletes, politicians, and many other people. "Each bottle is an ambassador for your country!" I said. Intense negotiations followed and ultimately both sides came to an understanding and the expansion took place. Catherine and I were guests at the opening of the new facilities. Today Fiji Water is the number one imported mineral water in the U.S., having displaced Evian. I remain proud of my small contribution towards its continued success and what that success has meant for the nation of Fiji.

I kept my eye on the tourism sector, too. Major American hotel chains like Sheraton, Hilton, and Outrigger had a large presence in Fiji and other boutique American resort operators like Club Wakaya and Turtle Island were also doing well. I wanted to encourage additional American chains, and worked to make certain that any enterprise investing American dollars in the country was being given a fair shake and treated within the bounds of international law. I worked to promote the continued introduction of cruise lines into Fiji, too, and urged Fiji tourism authorities to better develop the necessary amenities and infrastructure. Before I arrived, American Airlines had instituted nonstop flights from Los Angeles to Nadi, and I put forth efforts into expanding on that idea with other airlines, hoping to make Fiji not only a destination spot, but a hub for flights to Australia, New Zealand, and beyond.

Fiji certainly wasn't unknown to Americans. Motivational speaker Tony Robbins owned a resort in Fiji where he regularly packed in hundreds of his adherents. Malcolm Forbes owned an entire island called Laucala solely for his executive retreats. After he passed away, as per his wishes, he was buried there with a gravestone that reads: "While alive, he lived." Steve Forbes, his son, subsequently sold Laucala and my understanding from Fiji authorities is that he had to scramble to exhume Malcolm's body after the sale and have it shipped back to the States.

PAFCO, the Pacific Fishing Company, whose major customer was American-owned Bumble Bee tuna, had a major processing and canning plant on the island of Levuka. Catherine and I visited the plant and although the smell of the processing tuna was overwhelming, we were very impressed with the operation. Incidentally, the first consul-general of the U.S. to Fiji, John B. Williams, appointed by President Tyler in 1842, is buried on the island of Levuka.

One memorable incident was when I was told that an American couple running a small goldfish exporting business to the U.S. was facing closure because of a new government environmental decree. On my way to a meeting in Nadi one day, I decided to meet them at their operation. The couple were in their twenties and had developed this niche business all by themselves working arduously day and night. They loved their work and when they told me their story, they became very emotional. I promised to look into it for them and met with the minister in charge. Fortunately, I was able to restore the couple's license with ample environmental safeguards to accommodate the Fijians. It was especially gratifying to have successfully helped this young, industrious couple.

Another undertaking was my work with Voice of America, the U.S. government-funded broadcasting agency. We wanted to strengthen Fiji Broadcasting Corporation's radio frequency to the far-flung islands and arranged for the installation of a new satellite dish for that purpose. At the opening ceremony, attended by Minister Lekh Ram Vayeshnoi, I made a speech, saying, in part, "Democracy here and elsewhere ultimately depends upon an informed citizenry—citizens able to ponder and then help set the course of the nation. I represent a nation conceived in liberty. Over the course of two centuries, Americans have found that advancing democratic values and human rights serves our deepest values as well as our practical interest. Access to information is an important and vital part of the democratic process." I was also proud to speak at the opening of the new Fijian office for Habitat for Humanity, an organization founded in the United States in 1976 and which had built tens of thousands of homes in more than sixty countries.

One interesting experience, amusing in retrospect but somewhat embarrassing at the time, was my involvement in a major international drug bust. As it happens, I wasn't supposed to be involved. For several months, beginning in early 2000, the U.S. Drug Enforcement Administration, the FBI, the Royal Canadian Mounted Police, the Australian National Crime Authority, and New Zealand Customs, in collaboration with the Fiji Police Force had been working on an operation against suspected transnational drug criminals. A large drug syndicate was moving heroin—400 kilograms with a street value of over $100 million—from the so-called golden triangle of Burma, Thailand, and Cambodia, running it through China, and stockpiling it in Fiji for transshipment to the U.S., Canada, Australia, and New Zealand.

The international coalition of agencies had put together a highly secretive, highly sensitive operation, taking months of planning and coordination, that was going to culminate in a huge bust at the Ming Palace Restaurant in Suva on a Monday morning in October. The site was chosen because the owner of the restaurant was a part of the criminal ring.

A few days before, Catherine had to travel back home to the U.S. to visit her gravely ill father. I was doing double duty watching the kids, however poorly. On Sunday evening, I decided we'd all go out to dinner. I let go of my chauffeur and told the chef to take a break, too. Then the kids and I hopped in the car and out we went, only to find ourselves engaged in a heated discussion about the destination. Little Zack was adamant about going to

McDonald's while the others were split between Chinese and Japanese. Finally, after much negotiation for which all of my diplomatic skills were put to the test, it was agreed that we would pick up Zack's dinner from McDonald's and then go to a Chinese place where Zack could munch on his nuggets and fries and the rest of us could enjoy a nice Chinese meal. The restaurant of choice? Ming Palace.

In all the commotion, the imminent drug bust had totally escaped me. I'd been briefed on it, but had forgotten all about it. The whole restaurant was under surveillance with agents and sharpshooters placed at various vantage points outside. Imagine the consternation and anguish of those monitoring the situation after having spent months getting to such a critical point. I can hear them even now: *What the hell is the ambassador thinking?! He's going to blow our cover!* Happily, our dinner ended before the fireworks began and the operation went off very successfully the next morning as planned. Afterward, I invited all the agents and personnel involved to my office where I thanked them for their successful mission and we all had a good laugh about my Chinese dinner.

Early in 2001, a rather bizarre situation developed involving Tuvalu. Ron McMullen told me that he had just received some information that members of a spiritual movement led by Maharishi Mahesh Yogi were in the final stages of negotiations with the government of Tuvalu to purchase one of their islands where they would declare their own independent sovereign country, complete with its own government, flag, and currency. I had heard the name. Maharishi Mahesh Yogi was the head of the transcendental meditation movement, and one-time guru to the Beatles. Apparently, he was looking to build

a small, Vatican-like state as a headquarters for his organization, the Global Country of World Peace, and was offering $200
million to the Tuvaluan government, which was evidently sal-
ivating at the prospect. They wanted our reaction. Of course,
we were aghast. It was inconceivable to me that the government was even considering the idea of selling part of its small
country off. How naïve! I had Ron talk to the Tuvaluan ambassador and I spoke by phone with the prime minister, warning
him, politely, but firmly, of the dire consequences such actions
would invoke for his country. "Nations or sovereignty cannot
be bought or sold in the open bazaar," I told him. "You should
not even be thinking about this." Thankfully, reason prevailed
in the end and the "Independent Republic of Maharishi" never
materialized.

Embassy Suva's consular responsibilities included more
than the nations of Fiji, Tuvalu, Tonga, and Nauru. French
Polynesia—Tahiti, New Caledonia, and Wallis and Futuna—
also came under my purview. Tahiti, naturally, was a big
tourist destination for Americans, with over a hundred thousand
Americans descending on the Tahitian islands every year. Our
consular staff made periodic visits to Tahiti for routine visa and
consular work but it was emergencies like lost passports, illness,
or drowning that stretched the workload of my staff. I petitioned
the Department of State to set up a full-time consular office
in Papeete, the main city of Tahiti and the capital of French
Polynesia, which would help solve the problem.

In December of 1999, I was asked to be the co-leader of the
U.S. delegation to the first meeting of the Conference of the
Pacific Community, held in Tahiti. The conference adopted the
Tahiti Declaration that provided for the organizational setup and

service regulations for the Secretariat of the Pacific Community (SPC). The SPC is an international development organization, headquartered in Noumea, New Caledonia, and owned and governed by its twenty-six country and territory members, including the United States. The organization is focused on developmental issues within the context of the region, including climate change, disaster risk management, food security, gender equality, human rights, non-communicable disease prevention, and youth employment. After the conference, I traveled to the SPC headquarters in Noumea and was officially greeted by Director-General Lourdes Pangelinan who gave me a working tour of the facilities and a comprehensive briefing of the organization's diverse manifesto. I was pleased to reiterate to her the U.S. government's support of the SPC, and thanked her for her tremendous efforts to highlight many of the issues paramount to the organization.

In November 2000, I traveled back to Tahiti to review security cooperation and other bilateral matters. First, it was a stop in Wellington, New Zealand where I'd been invited to attend a regional conference. Catherine accompanied me. Also invited was CINCPAC Admiral Blair who brought his wife Dianne along. The conference in Wellington went well, and we also had just enough time to get a quick glimpse of this beautiful capital city.

After that, the four of us took a flight to Papeete. But this was no ordinary flight. We boarded a military Boeing 707 specially modified for the CINCPAC himself, and piloted by him. We took off from a New Zealand Air Force base and I was able to take in an extraordinary view of the expansive Pacific from the vantage point of the cockpit. The landing at the Papeete airport was dramatic, to say the least. There seemed to be nothing below us but crystal blue water. Then Denny descended toward a little dot in the sea and as we went lower, that dot became Tahiti. On the 707, with a single airstrip to accommodate us, it felt a little like landing on a postage stamp. After landing, we all enjoyed the colorful welcome reception accorded to the CINCPAC and the American ambassador. The French Navy pulled out all stops for us, which included a lilting Polynesian dance routine by some of the beautiful island girls.

During the conference, we carved out a day for sightseeing. Denny decided that he'd like to do some island hopping and the French Navy was ready with a helicopter for just that purpose. The four of us boarded and Denny asked the pilot to take us to the island of Moorea to pay a visit to Marlon Brando, who had an exclusive residence on that island. We flew straight there and hovered around his estate for a while, finally determining that the occupants weren't home. Denny and I were disappointed by not being able to catch up with Brando, but the disappointment was more palpable in the faces of Dianne and Catherine. Nonetheless, we flew on, settling for another island where cabanas, lunch, and music had been prearranged for us by the French Navy. It was an absolutely delightful day spent in one of the most beautiful spots on this earth.

Sadly, in my time as ambassador, I never made it to Wallis and Futuna, two islands dominated by two families, and with a combined population of around 11,000. There was one flight a week from New Zealand to Wallis; otherwise, it was about a week by boat. We scheduled an annual visit there by one of our consular officers. I simply never had the time or opportunity to make it there myself.

Those were interesting times for my family and me, to say the least. But back when I'd first arrived, in late 1999, as my work was just getting underway, changes were afoot. In Fiji, to be sure. But also around the world. After all, we were only months away from not only a new year, a new decade, or new century; we were about to enter a new millennium.

CHAPTER THIRTEEN

A New Millennium

THE THING ABOUT FIJI IS that it's just west of the International Date Line. What does this mean? Well, it means that every morning, the sun first rises over Fiji's shores. Fiji wakes up before the rest of the world. It's the first place on earth to experience the new day, the new year, or, in the case of the year 2000, the new millennium.

This created some real excitement towards the end of 1999, and by December 30, the excitement was considerable. Among other remarkable developments, a cruise ship docked in Suva filled with star-studded celebrities, all arriving to be the first to welcome 2000. One of those famous people was none other than Buzz Aldrin, the second man to walk on the moon. I welcomed Buzz and his wife to Fiji with an invitation to our residence.

Also present was Bill Bodde, former ambassador to Fiji, and his wife, and we all had an enjoyable time chatting. Despite his otherworldly career in space, I found Buzz to be genuine and down to earth. That night Catherine and I saw him again at a dinner, to which the captain invited us on board the cruise ship. We sat next to the Aldrins at the captain's table and I thought to myself what a colorful way the year was ending.

The following day, another cruise line held a gala picnic on the small island of Nukulau, just a few miles off of Suva. Buzz was the guest of honor and throngs of people gathered just to get a glimpse of him or to shake his hand. Touching Buzz Aldrin was as good as touching the moon! Our children were there, too, and were as enthralled as anyone else to be in the presence of this famous astronaut.

But not all was merriment. Our office had a rather serious piece of business to address. Being on the cusp of the new millennium meant we were also on the cusp of the Y2K crisis. Computers back then had been programmed with only two digits to represent the year. On January 1, the fear was that computers around the world would recognize the year 2000 as "00." This would theoretically cause widespread computer crashes. The internet and all communications would break down. Planes would fall out of the sky, ATMs would fail and banks would crash, power plants would stop producing power and the grid would go dark. It would be nothing less than a cyber-apocalypse.

Leading up to the millennium, billions of dollars had been spent around the world re-programming computers. Nevertheless, nobody really knew what was going to happen at 12:01 on January 1, 2000. Sitting practically on top of the International Date Line, we would be the first to know. From our embassy's unique vantage point, at ground zero, as it were, we were tasked with monitoring the situation and reporting to the U.S. government. Toward this end, we'd been given a lengthy to-do list that essentially added up to this: forget about the New Year festivities and keep your nose to the ground. Deputy Chief of Mission Ron McMullen rose to the occasion, as he always did, and took control of the task at hand. Of course, the world didn't end and the dire predictions turned out to be off the mark, fortunately.

At 12:01, instead of hunkering down waiting for the end-of-days, Catherine and I were helping to drive the final nails into a group of ten houses being built by Habitat for Humanity at a nearby village. Twenty-five volunteers from the United States, together with volunteers from Canada, Guam, and other local villages, had come to assist. The houses, each twenty-five feet by seventeen feet, with showers, toilets, and electricity, would be sold to needy homeowners at cost, with a monthly payment of thirty dollars over a ten-year period. Most of the funding for these "Millennium Homes" came from the U.S.

I provided the dedication speech, saying "Habitat for Humanity is building more than just houses. Habitat builds hopes, bonds of friendship, and bridges between different communities." I also extolled the more general idea that philanthropy was one of the secrets behind America's overall welfare. I urged wealthy Fijians to engage in philanthropy, too. "America was built on the foundations of responsive, responsible communities," I said. "That means support for those less fortunate and recognition of their needs that must be fulfilled."

At the conclusion of the event, Catherine and I rushed home so we could change for a dazzling black-tie New Year's affair thrown by Tia Barrett, the New Zealand high commissioner. Barrett was the first Maori chief to hold that position. At the party, everyone had a great time welcoming the new millennium until the wee hours of the morning.

But this was just the beginning of the millennium celebrations. Catherine and I decided that we needed to make Fiji join America as it welcomed the new year some twelve hours later. We had planned a millennium party at the residence, installing huge, widescreen TVs for guests to view the festivities as they'd get underway around the world. We had run into a serious problem, however. None of the audio-visual equipment and accessories we wanted were available in Fiji. The nearest place to rent them was Australia. Since a millennium comes around only once every one-thousand years, I decided to go for it, shipping in all the electronic equipment we needed. Then we'd erected a huge tent to house the giant outdoor TV screens. Three food stalls had been set up with American, Fijian, and Indian cuisine. A local band had been hired to entertain the crowd with live music.

My admin officer had shown up in my office one morning leading up to the blowout. She ran through the arrangements with the accompanying cost. Her unspoken words: *Who's going to pay for all this?* The embassy's representational allowances weren't enough to pay for even one-tenth of the expense. I put her mind to ease. "Millenniums don't come too often," I said. "It will be my pleasure to take care of the party for this one!" I could see the relief in her eyes.

The party started in earnest. Before the ball dropped at New York's Times Square, the entire tent was teeming with our guests. Prime Minister Mahendra Chaudhry showed up with his family, as did his entire cabinet. Judges, institutional heads, civic and business leaders, diplomats, and many other dignitaries and friends attended. At times, there was standing room only. It was the most important show in town that evening, and everybody was having a great time. After the New York City ball dropped, it was Chicago's turn, and then Las Vegas, finally wrapping things up in Honolulu. We watched it all on the big-screen TVs and toasted with each celebration. Everyone seemed to voice the same sentiment: Fiji had never quite seen anything like this before. Nobody left until the end and when they did leave, and we had said our goodbyes and thanked everyone for coming, Catherine and I fell exhausted into our bed.

As the year 2000 got underway, I began hitting my stride, becoming well- acclimated to my routine. Though Fiji was not necessarily on the frontline of world events, there was nonetheless a constant barrage of day-to-day activities to keep Embassy Suva busy with important issues. One of my priorities was to enhance US-Fiji trade, a process I labeled "aggressive commercial outreach." I implored all businesses to engage in trade and commerce by getting online. Addressing the Pacific Asia Travel Association, I described the importance of the rapidly developing internet. "The new truth for destination marketing organizations is that if you are not online, then you are not on sale within your key markets," I said. "The web is the new destination marketing battleground and if you are not in there fighting, then you cannot expect to win the battle for tourist dollars." This was long before the proliferation of the likes of Priceline, Orbitz, Expedia, TripAdvisor, and other dot-com travel companies. I could see where the industry was headed and I made it my mission to make others see it, too.

Speaking to the Fiji-US Business Council, I encouraged entrepreneurship, citing the modest beginnings of American business leaders like Bill Gates and Steve Jobs. "The basics of the American model of market competition is being adopted by countries around the world. This is one of the reasons why prosperity for global growth has never been brighter." But I made it clear that there was no such thing as a benign or a benevolent investor. Fiji may have beautiful shores and sunshine, but that wouldn't be enough for investment dollars to flow in. Investors seek return on their investment, for which they also need solid institutions and political stability.

One particularly impressive Fijian enterprise that served as the perfect example of what Fijians could accomplish was the Tappoo group of companies, headed by Kanti Tappoo, OBE (Officer of the Order of the British Empire). Kanti was an Indo-Fijian entrepreneur of extraordinary charm, acumen, and leadership. Kanti's vast enterprise, including retail, manufacturing, and hospitality concerns, employed thousands of Fijians, embracing all values, and was on the cutting edge of contemporary digital technology. I got to know Kanti and was honored to call him my friend.

In early March, I received a message from the White House that President Clinton wanted me to accompany him as a member of his cabinet delegation on his upcoming state visits to India and Bangladesh. This was beyond my expectations, and I greatly appreciated the kind and thoughtful gesture by the president. Going back to Bangladesh, the place of my birth, as an American ambassador with the president of the United States would truly be a landmark event for me.

We arrived in New Delhi, India, March 19, 2000, and left

for Dhaka, Bangladesh early Monday morning March 20 on the first leg of the combined state visit. Our special air force plane arrived at Dhaka airport around noon with a delegation which, besides the president, included the secretaries of state and commerce, the national security advisor, the chief of staff to the president, the press secretary to the president, seven congressional members from both parties, the USAID director, and the chief of protocol, among others, for a grand total of eighty-six members of the president's entourage.

After the welcoming ceremony, came the receiving line. I was the fourth person after Madeleine Albright, Richard Daley, and John Podesta, to be introduced by President Clinton to the President of Bangladesh Justice Shahabuddin Ahmed and Prime Minister Sheikh Hasina. This was a singularly unique moment in my life. I was representing America, my homeland, as an official guest in the country that was my motherland. And I had come while accompanying President Clinton on the first-ever visit by any U.S. president. I wondered what thoughts went through the minds of the Bangladesh president and prime minister as I shook their hands. If they could have read my thoughts, they would have perceived nothing but wonderment for the circumstances in which I found myself.

The motorcade left the airport and I noticed that all the streets were lined with thousands and thousands of onlookers waving U.S. and Bangladesh flags. Many of them were school children in their uniforms, which led me to presume that schools and offices had decided to close early for the day.

Our first stop was a news conference with Prime Minister Sheikh Hasina in front of her office. One of the questions posed to President Clinton had to do with undocumented Bangladeshis living in the U.S. "Do you want to make your visit memorable by declaring a general amnesty for them?" said the inquirer.

"I have done what I can to make sure that none are unfairly treated," President Clinton replied. "We have laws that govern this...but I said in my opening statement, and I will say it again, I think our country has been greatly enriched by the presence of Bangladeshis, and we have many Bangladeshi-American citizens. One of them is here with me today—Osman Siddique, who's our ambassador to Fiji. And so, I feel very good about the presence of Bangladeshis within the United States. But I have to observe the laws that we have."

Afterward, the president had other scheduled bilateral discussions with Bangladesh government officials, and I went off with Commerce Secretary William Daly and other congressional members to a meeting/lunch hosted by the commerce minister of Bangladesh, Mr. Tofail Ahmed. Coincidentally, I knew Minister Ahmed back when he was a respected student-leader of the Bangladesh independence movement. A bold and charismatic speaker, he'd been at the forefront of the movement. Now, he was one of the most capable and effective cabinet members in the government.

Next was a closed-door meeting between President Clinton, Secretary Albright, National Security Advisor Sandy Berger, and other senior members of the delegation, and the leader of the opposition, Khaleda Zia. It was no secret that the relationship between the prime minister and the opposition leader was at times hostile. The press had dubbed the pair "the dueling begums," begum being the colloquial term for female leader or aristocrat. The meeting was intended to smooth things between the two women and end the parliamentary boycott by the opposition leader. Secretary Albright, a diplomat and negotiator of immense stature, came out of the meeting looking frustrated and disappointed. I could see that despite all her efforts and persuasive powers, progress had not been made.

The final stop was the state dinner, hosted by President Shahabuddin Ahmed at the opulent presidential mansion. My name was announced and I was introduced to the Bangladesh president. President Clinton, standing next to him, smiled at me, took my hand, and said, "Osman, are you having a good time?"

"This is surreal, Mr. President," I answered. "Thank you very much." It was all I could think of to say, so honored was I by the opportunity.

After the elaborate banquet, punctuated by a cultural show, we all rushed back to the airport and boarded our airplane around midnight for New Delhi. The next day began with the more colorful India portion of the visit. Chelsea Clinton, the president's daughter, and Dorothy Rodham, his mother-in-law, joined the entourage. I was introduced to them by my friend Huma Abedin. Huma, a Pakistani-American was an elegant, energetic, and effective special assistant to the first lady. I continued to maintain my relationship with her when she later became a senior aide to Senator Clinton, deputy chief of staff to Secretary Clinton, and later campaign vice-chair to Hillary's 2016 presidential bid. Huma has always been accessible and helpful to me and the friendship continues to this day.

We were all housed at the Maurya Sheraton, which was, quite literally, taken over by U.S. security and secret service personnel. It became fortress-like and getting in and out on your own was not a simple task. In one of our official rides to the city, I could not miss a big banner blazing, "Welcome Chelsea!

Thanks for bringing your dad!" The sign reminded me of a line JFK spoke to the French press during a state visit to Paris in 1961. "I do not think it altogether inappropriate for me to introduce myself," Kennedy said. "I am the man who accompanied Jacqueline Kennedy to Paris."

The welcome accorded to us by President Kocheril Raman Narayanan and Prime Minister Atul Bihari Vajpayee was extraordinary, steeped in Indian culture and tradition. Our time was consumed by meetings and receptions with businesses and other political leaders. U.S. Ambassador Richard Celeste hosted a luncheon at the Roosevelt House, his official residence. There, I had the opportunity to meet with opposition leader Sonia Gandhi and her two young children Rahul and Priyanka.

Our itinerary called for a scheduled visit to Raj Ghat, a memorial dedicated to honor Mahatma Gandhi. It's a black marble platform with an eternal flame that marks the spot where Mahatma Gandhi was cremated on January 30, 1948, a day after his assassination. Our group arrived before President Clinton's motorcade did. As is the custom at Raj Ghat, you must take off your shoes and put on white cotton slippers, which are provided to you. I tried several until I found a pair that fit me. When the president arrived, the Raj Ghat staff tried several pairs of slippers on him, but not even the largest fit his feet. Seeing the distress and embarrassment on their faces, the president decided to abandon the exercise and walk barefoot, thus avoiding any show of disrespect to their tradition. At that moment, I also decided to discard my perfectly fitted slippers and I walked barefoot alongside the president and Chelsea. The visit was solemn and as President Clinton bowed his head, we all followed suit, showing our respect to the great man who was Mahatma Gandhi.

The trip was nothing less than amazing to me. But once back in Suva, I had to quickly get myself back into the normal swing of things. Not all was well. I was beginning to feel a distinct air of dissonance permeating the political atmosphere of the city. It seemed that Prime Minister Chaudhary had revived some old racial wounds and kindled a very sensitive subject in Fiji: land ownership.

I started looking for an opportunity to address the issue to a large audience and soon found one. I was invited to be the chief guest and main speaker at the opening of the SANGAM (the India Sanmarga Ikya Sangam) convention, held annually in Suva, the largest gathering in the country of Hindu Indo-Fijians, numbering close to 5,000. On April 21, 2000, I found myself at the national stadium in Suva, which was packed with a large, attentive crowd of Indo-Fijians, diplomats, media, and civic and political leaders. Upon my arrival, the waiting host committee asked me, perhaps because I was a Muslim, if they could welcome me with their traditional Hindu ritual. "Of course, you can," I said. There were lighted wickers and candles, and incenses swirled around my face. Then the ceremonial red dot was placed on my forehead.

In my speech, I extolled the contribution Indo-Fijians made toward the development of the country. Quoting from President Ratu Mara's book, *The Pacific Way*, I said, "There is only one way for this nation to go. We must all find a common path towards unity, a unity that transcends race and religion and recognizes that we are all sons and daughters of Fiji." I added that all the Fiji communities had to come together to build a stronger and prosperous future for their children. Giving America's example of growing diversity of race and religion, I said that Fiji had a chance for a better history and better race relations, if—and only if—everyone participated. "Fiji getting back to reconciliation, economic growth, and prosperity, and becoming a full participant in the twenty-first-century global village is in everyone's interest. If Fiji doesn't get back on track, it will have only itself to blame. Yes, we will help in any and every way possible, but the healing, the willingness to accept changes, must come from within. The past one-hundred years have seen victory of freedom over totalitarianism. But still around us, we see failure to use our freedom wisely, as too many people give in to primitive hatred, and we still face the oldest problem: the fear of those different from us. History shows that people do tend to be afraid of those who don't look the same or practice the same religion or come from different tribes or have different lifestyles. Those fears, when ignited and organized by unscrupulous leaders, have led to terrible violence in the modern world." When I concluded, the stadium stood up in a roar of applause that continued for several minutes. As Catherine and I were departing, we were showered with rose petals and kind words. But would my spoken thoughts that day make a difference?

In the time I'd been in Fiji, I had developed a warm and cordial relationship with Frank Bainimarama based on mutual respect and trust. Similarly, his wife Maria and Catherine became good friends. One day in April, I invited Frank over to the house for drinks and some heart-to-heart chat. He showed up around 11:00 p.m., driving his military SUV himself and with no security. We decided to sit outside in the sprawling veranda of the British-colonial residence, surrounded by exotic tropical plants and scented flowers. There was a calm gentle wind blowing, making the evening most relaxing.

Frank was a down-to-earth person and after long hours at work, he apparently welcomed this respite. The discussion centered on Fiji's brewing political unease. Frank was candid and objective that evening, which validated the conclusions I had come to about his character and commitment. At that particular moment, I found in Frank a patriot, supportive of Fiji's nascent democracy, uninterested in usurping power, and determined to keep the military inside the barracks. He was a good soldier. Nevertheless, Frank sounded some alarm bells over the prevailing situation in his country. I could not help but be concerned about the overall situation. Frank stayed way beyond midnight as we mixed lighthearted banter with serious discussion. The next day, I conveyed my thoughts about our conversation to Washington.

In early May, I was invited to inaugurate the twenty-eighth annual congress of the Fiji Institute of Accountants, a highly influential economic body. On the economic front, I was concerned with the Fiji government's market intervention and the lack of transparency in its decision-making. Delivering my keynote address, I decided to hit hard on those issues in front of a record number of delegates, government officials, diplomats, press members, and other invited guests. "The United States Government has real concerns regarding agricultural trade policies of the Fiji Government," I began. "And it supports Australia's initiative in the World Trade Organization to question Fiji's recent imposition of a rice quota. We believe such steps are not consistent with Fiji's commitments to the World Trade Organization and will lead to higher prices for rice here, and lower quality and less choice for consumers. We are concerned that Fiji may impose bans on poultry imports or change its present agreement with the U.S. Such steps could be construed as barriers to trade and could be another issue for WTO review. It is particularly important for economies in transition, such as in Fiji, that government and business develop and establish a positive public-private partnership. Government's role should be to facilitate and encourage entrepreneurship and not frustrate business. As a rule, the less interference by government the better. And to be frank, at the present time, I know that several businesses here and overseas are frustrated about doing business in Fiji. My own government has concerns about certain decisions taken with respect to economic and commercial policy."

After the speech, I was practically mobbed by the press and would have loved to take more than the few questions I took but had to rush home to pick up Catherine and leave for the airport. We were headed to the Island of Lau in celebration of President Ratu Mara's eightieth birthday. In the previous few decades, major transformation had taken place throughout many of the island nations as they had moved from colonialism to independence. These small nations were developing a newfound sense of national identity as a unified regional entity in the modern, complex world. Fiji's President, Ratu Sir Kamisese Mara, had played a significant role in this transition for his people. To honor this great leader, statesman, and paramount chief, thousands were gathering in Tubou, Lakeba, and Lau to celebrate his birthday.

Catherine and I joined many members of the diplomatic corps to show our respect. We witnessed the colorful presentations and ritualistic Kava ceremonies, and later participated in dancing and singing. I came to learn that President Mara enjoyed the National Geographic series on TV and so I arranged to get the entire library of all past episodes, which I presented to the president as our gift. He burst into a wide smile and said, "This should take care of all of my evenings until my eighty-fifth birthday!"

Back in Suva, I wanted to get a better grip on the political situation. I met with journalists, politicians, and cross-sections of civic leaders. I met with Sir James Ah Koy, a Chinese-Fijian who was former finance minister in the Rabuka government, an opposition parliamentarian, and the owner of the U.S. Embassy building on Loftus Street. Sir James was an especially successful businessman, an astute politician, and a very good friend of mine. He raised some issues which were of concern to me and of which I took note. But one of the more telling meetings was with the leader of the opposition in parliament, Ratu Inoke Kubuabola. He was extremely critical of many of the prime minister's policies, especially when it came to indigenous rights. He felt thoroughly disparaged by the P.M.'s son, Rajendra, a member of the prime minister's official inner circle who, Kubuabola said, had been going to extraordinary lengths to deprive him of a smooth-functioning opposition leader's office. He'd been given no secretary, no assistant, outdated computers, and a used car that was well-worn. He'd felt disrespected and for good reason in my estimation. I knew then that I needed to have a meeting with Prime Minister Mahendra Chaudhry, the sooner the better.

Fortunately, the opportunity came right away. Two senior executives of the Outrigger hotel chain in Hawaii were in town and visited with me. Outrigger already had a major presence in Fiji but came with another significant project for the country—a comprehensive package to rehab, renovate, and upgrade the boarded-up Grand Pacific Hotel in Suva. The hotel, known as "The Grand Old Lady" was located on the main seafront on Victoria Parade. In its heyday, the Grand Pacific was in the same league as the Raffles Hotel in Singapore and the Peninsula in Hong Kong. Distinguished guests had included Somerset Maugham, Sir Charles Kingsford Smith, and James A. Michener. Queen Elizabeth II and Prince Phillip are known to have stayed at the hotel on a few occasions.

I liked the Outrigger presentation and thought it would provide a good segue by which to meet with the prime minister. When my office called the P.M.'s office, we were told that since the parliament was in session, Mahendra Chaudhry was not attending office at the secretariat, spending most of the days and evenings at Parliament House. How about meeting him during recess at his office at Parliament? I suggested. That idea was met with agreement and we were given a time to have a working lunch with the prime minister at his office on Tuesday, May 16. The Outrigger folks were elated and when the lunch meeting came, they gave Chaudhry a short but very impressive presentation.

Following that, I asked for some private time with the prime minister. I had met him before, of course. My very first meeting with Chaudhry actually took place before I'd met President Mara to present my credentials. To me, Chaudhry was something of an enigma. On a personal level, I found him to be engaging, soft-spoken, and a very smart politician. His public persona, on the other hand, was quite different. He could be arrogant and combative, a style more appropriate to the labor movement from which he came than to the parliament he was elected to lead. Despite his outward pretense of bravado, he'd requested of me an electronic sweep of his office complex to determine if his predecessor had bugged it. A team of technical experts periodically came in from Embassy Canberra to do routine security, cyber, and telecommunications checks on all our premises and to review the security measures in place at all our facilities. On their subsequent mission to Suva, I had to pull some major strings to accommodate the prime minister's unorthodox request. Happily, nothing was found. Another time, when I had invited Chaudhry to lunch at the residence, he'd asked me if we could get him an armored car like mine. It was obvious he was not comfortable with his own security and intelligence set up. Of course, I politely turned down this second request.

Meeting with Chaudhry after the Outrigger meeting, I asked him if he was aware of any dissatisfaction among the ethnic Fijians. I pressed further, wanting to know if he had any specific intel on a protest march that was scheduled to take place in Suva the coming Friday. The prime minister, in his characteristic nonchalant manner, discounted the prospect of any such threats, calmly dismissing any danger as a "Fijian myth." Nonetheless, I suggested that he carefully take notice of the growing complaints by a significant section of the population. Additionally, I implored him to recognize the legitimacy of the opposition in parliament, which, I reminded him, is essential to the proper functioning of a parliamentary democracy. At one point, I told him, "Mr. Prime Minister, your forefathers came to this country from India as indentured laborers only about a hundred years ago. How historic and wonderful it is to see that the people of Fiji have given you this golden opportunity to govern for a term of five years. Please take your time fixing any of your past inequalities. The people of Fiji have put their trust in your leadership and judgment." He smiled and thanked me for bringing the Outrigger opportunity and assured me that he would consider the issues I raised with him.

Three days later, that Friday morning, May 19, 2000, when parliament was in full session and the prime minister and his entire cabinet were in attendance, the fate of Fiji would change dramatically.

CHAPTER FOURTEEN

Turmoil in Paradise

MAY 19, 2000. CATHERINE CAME clean about my surprise fiftieth birthday party when I called to tell her of the coup. Our residence was two blocks from the parliament building, the epicenter of the chaos. She'd heard gunfire. "Yes, I was planning a surprise party," she cried, "but I hadn't ordered fireworks!"

Catherine's immediate concern was the kids at school. Moments earlier, I had called the principal of the school, which was located on the outskirts of the city, and apprised him of the mayhem going on in Suva. I told him that a team of embassy personnel was headed towards the school and to make sure, in the meantime, that the perimeter of the school was fully secured. I assured Catherine of the kids' safety and asked her to take necessary precautions herself at home. I mentioned the safety drills we were acquainted with and reminded her of the residence's safe room.

Then I called Stanley Roth, Assistant Secretary of the Bureau of East Asian and Pacific Affairs. Since our standard telephone connections had been disrupted, I had to make the call from the rooftop of the embassy building, utilizing a makeshift satellite link. The connection was scratchy and I'd apparently caught Stan at an odd hour. I explained to him the situation: "Stan, reports are that the government has been overthrown by some combination of paramilitary and local militia elements. The entire cabinet, including the prime minister, has been taken hostage inside the parliament building. At this point, their fate is unknown. As I speak, the whole place is being overrun by radical and criminal elements. I see smoke billowing out from buildings, and roads are being blocked with burning tires and fallen trees. There are masses of people running amok in the street with guns, machetes, firebombs, rocks, and everything else lethal. It looks like a lot of Indian-owned shops and restaurants are being burned and looted. There are no signs of any first responders or police anywhere."

"What?" he replied. "Listen, hold on for a moment." There was a short pause and then Stan came back to the line. "Ambassador," he said, "you have to reverse this situation."

My mind raced. Reverse the situation? *Reverse the situation?* I tried to think of something to say that wouldn't sound sarcastic, or worse. Reversing situations like paramilitary coups wasn't exactly in my briefing papers.

Before I could reply, Stan said, "Give me a few minutes." Then he hung up and I waited for him to call back with something I hoped would be a little more helpful. Ten minutes later he rang back, sounding much more composed and deliberate. "Where is General Rabuka?" he asked, referencing the former P.M. and leader of the 1987 coup. "Please get a hold of him and determine his movements. Also, is President Mara okay? Connect with him and make sure he is still functioning." There were a few additional details, both general and classified, and we ended the call.

Over at the school, meanwhile, our convoy had arrived, but Captain Brent Barker, our regional security officer, found the place to be in chaos. After receiving my call, the principal had sounded the high-alert bell. The lali gong, a traditional wooden gong, had been in full swing and panicked students and teachers had been running helter-skelter all over the place. Our eldest son, Omar, a senior at the school, had the presence of mind to gather all the American students into a secure room to await help. Later, he would admit to me that he felt awful not being able to help evacuate the others—his Aussie, Kiwi, and Fijian friends. But the place was in pandemonium and there were only so many vehicles from our embassy to whisk the students away.

Back at the embassy, we were in full-crisis mode. My first responsibility was to make sure all the embassy personnel and staff were safe and secure and their movements carefully planned and monitored. The "warden" system was activated, which essentially alerted all Americans living in Fiji of the crisis and gave them specific guidelines while advising extreme caution. Approximately 3,500 Americans, mostly retirees and business owners, lived on the Fiji islands. A twenty-four-hour link with the DOS operations center in D.C. was established. I asked Ron McMullen to quickly locate General Rabuka and bring him over to my office at the earliest opportunity.

The day ended without any clear idea as to where the events of the coup were headed. I stayed late with my emergency team and then finally went home to my family. Catherine and I had a quiet dinner of Italian food that had been slated for my birthday party. Most of the food, she had earlier boxed up and sent to the embassy staff. I didn't eat well and slept that night even worse. Outside, we could hear the mobs of people in the street and I was thankful for our security team.

The opportunity to speak with General Rabuka came the next day. Ron had tracked him down and he made his way to the embassy. Phyllis Williams, my executive assistant, opened the door to my office and there Rabuka stood—a stocky middle-aged man with a thick mustache. Both his hands were raised. "Not guilty!" he said in his loud, commanding, general's voice. "I didn't do it!"

I stifled a laugh and ushered him inside. We chatted and Rabuka quickly disavowed any involvement in the overthrow of the government and he assured me of his fullest cooperation in resolving the crisis. I took his assurances with a grain of salt, however. We had some intel about recent activities on his island that involved him and certain retired military officers and tribal leaders. We had no evidence of his involvement with the coup, but I decided to keep him on my radar and closely monitored.

What we would quickly learn was that a U.S.-educated Fijian businessman by the name of George Speight was behind the coup. Speight claimed to be a champion of indigenous rights and came along at just the right time. Resentment had been brewing, just as I'd warned Prime Minister Chaudhry. Chaudhry had dismissed it as a "Fijian myth." Speight, however, was no champion of indigenous rights. He was a disgruntled, mediocre businessman making a power play and he'd somehow managed to muster up support from some former soldiers and certain members of the military.

Meanwhile, with Prime Minister Chaudhry held hostage, I wanted to talk to President Mara, but his office was slow to accept my request for an appointment. I was told he was not keeping well. I kept the pressure on and two days after the coup, we were finally told we could see him. I was accompanied by Ron and a contingent of my armed security detail. As we approached the Government House, I recalled my last visit there to present my credentials. It looked eerily different now. The big iron gate at the entrance was padlocked with thick chains. The security guards looked tired and confused. Apparently, I was the first visitor to enter through the gates since the coup.

We waited a short while in the president's private anteroom and soon the president came in. It had been only a week since his eightieth birthday celebration, but he looked like a shadow of the man I'd toasted on that occasion. His six-foot, five-inch frame seemed smaller. He walked in with a slight stoop, his radiant smile gone. His handshake was weak and his voice low. I asked him how he was doing. "Coping as best as I can under the circumstances," he said.

I reiterated my government's strong condemnation of the coup and its leaders and voiced my concern at the demise of Fiji's nascent democracy. Our bilateral relations would face imminent disruption. Our military-to-military cooperation would be suspended. And my efforts to bring back the Peace Corps (his special request) would be aborted. Mara stared down at the floor saying nothing.

I then presented him with two options to consider, subject to his formal request of the U.S. government. First, I offered him the support of our trained hostage negotiating team, to be flown in from the States to help resolve the situation. The second option was to invite an elite force to smash through the barriers the hostage-takers had set up and recover and release the hostages. With respect to the first option, he deferred. The crisis needed to be resolved by Fijians themselves, the "Pacific way," he said. In mulling over the second option, he asked if there would be any casualties or fatalities. I said yes, the possibility was always there; nobody could guarantee the total safety of all lives in such an operation. After my answer, I noticed tears beginning to run down his cheeks. President Mara's own daughter, Adi Koila, a cabinet minister, was one of the hostages. The thought of such an operation was unacceptable to him. I understood his dilemma and didn't push the matter any further.

Before we parted, President Mara took me aside and voiced concerns about his own personal safety and the safety of his wife. I offered my residence's official guest quarters as a safe haven. He thanked me and said he'd consider my invitation. He never availed himself of it, but I think he felt safer knowing the option was there.

On May 22, United Nations Secretary-General Kofi Annan dispatched Sergio Viera de Mello, serving at that time as the U.N. administrator in East Timor, to Fiji as his special envoy. De Mello was accompanied by Don McKinnon, the Commonwealth secretary-general. Upon arrival in Suva, de Mello sought a one-on-one meeting with me, which we held over breakfast at his hotel. I apprised him of the situation, as well as the events leading to the overthrow of the government. Then we both gave a statement to the waiting press about the dire consequences of this forceful takeover of a democratically elected government that went against all international norms and practices. Fiji would have to pay a huge price, both domestically and internationally, for this misadventure. McKinnon, in fact, would announce that Fiji's expulsion from the Commonwealth was imminent.

De Mello later visited with coup leader George Speight in the parliament building where he was holding all the hostages, but nothing came of this meeting. Before he left Suva, de Mello recalled to me with great pride his work as a young professional with the United Nations High Commission for Refugees in the 1971 Bangladesh war of independence. We talked for quite a while. I enjoyed my time with Sergio and found him to be intelligent and dedicated. I would remember our short time together a few years later. On August 19, 2003, Sergio Viera de Mello would be killed in Baghdad, Iraq in the Canal Hotel bombing where he was serving as the United Nations Special Representative. Twenty members of his staff would be killed along with him. In 2004, the government of Fiji would become the first country to agree to provide troops specifically to protect U.N. officials in Iraq.

A week after de Mello's visit to Fiji, on May 29, President Mara resigned from office under disputed circumstances. Speight swore in ruling government member Timoci Silatolu as prime minister, and proclaimed Jope Seniloli president. But it was largely symbolic. Support for Speight's coup only went so far. For all intents and purposes, the coup had created a power vacuum. Stepping into it was none other than Commodore Frank Bainimarama, who announced on radio and television that he had taken over the government and declared martial law. Then he abrogated the constitution the following day and proceeded to appoint an interim government.

Meanwhile, Speight's group continued to hold Chaudhry and his cabinet ministers hostage. In a television interview on June 8, broadcast by the world media, including CNN, I branded George Speight a terrorist and said he should be brought to trial. "I don't think he should get immunity. He is a common criminal, a terrorist, and justice should be served to him." Apparently, Speight saw the interview and became infuriated by what I'd said. He and his cohorts considered me "persona non grata" and credible threats were subsequently made against me. The DOS was worried about my personal security and measures were taken to bolster it. Admiral Blair called me from Honolulu and reassured me of his assistance, if needed. Soon after, State ordered an evacuation of all American families and non-essential embassy personnel.

My family left for Virginia and, along with a select few senior staff members, I stayed behind to manage the situation under heavy security. Many evenings, RSO Captain Barker would show up and, based on threat levels, would take me to various undisclosed locations to spend the night. Normally, I sleep poorly in new surroundings and I must admit that those nights were long and lonely.

One night was particularly tense. Lynne Gadkowski was a junior foreign service officer doing her first tour of duty as an American diplomat at embassy Suva. A graduate of Cornell University, Lynne passed the foreign service exams, got her FSI training, and was posted to my embassy as third secretary, vice-consul. She was bright and energetic and livened up any social occasion. As per official guidelines, she was allocated a fully furnished house, a beautiful bungalow overlooking the ocean and surrounded by a well-manicured tropical garden. Not bad for a twenty-four-year-old single girl on her first overseas assignment.

Late one night, way past midnight, I got a frantic call from Lynne. It seemed her house had been caught in a crossfire between rebels and government troops. Bands of men armed with weapons were about to crash through her gate and get to her front door. I asked her to stay calm and make sure she knew of an alternate exit. We were under a dusk to dawn curfew and I was alone at the house. Taking advantage of the curfew, my driver was off duty. I got a hold of the car keys and asked my personal armed security to accompany me. Thinking about the evasive driving lessons I'd had during my orientation in D.C., we headed straight for Lynne's house, about a ten-minute drive from my residence. Mine was the only armored car in the country, nicknamed the "Yank Tank," and I had a tough Fijian as my wingman! I drove through both army and rebel lines with blinkers on, horns blazing, and with American flags in full sight.

We entered Lynne's property, jumped out of the car, and quickly scoped the perimeter. We saw no one and heard nothing. I shouted for Lynne. No response. Then, as we were about to enter the house, I saw Lynne hunkered down in an outside ditch silhouetted by the bushes, understandably shaken. I asked her to clean up, pack, and hop in the car with me. For the next several weeks, she stayed at the guest quarters of our residence.

On June 25, four female hostages were released. On June 28, sixteen journalists, an American among them, were detained by Speight after a press conference. Speight told them he could not guarantee their safety outside the parliament building and that military leaders had ordered their soldiers to shoot to kill. He advised them to spend the night in the parliament building and some of the journalists sensed they were about to become hostages themselves.

When I got word of this, I knew we needed to act immediately, not just for the sake of the American, although that would have been sufficient reason for action, but also for the principles of a free press. One of the best things about America is the First Amendment and I knew, as Ambassador representing my country, that I needed to convey the value of an unfettered (perhaps literally) press.

On my direction, Ron McMullen made a direct phone call to the hostage-takers. He was put on speaker so the coup leaders and the journalists could hear our message "not to mess with America." Ron declared, "If the journalists are not released within twenty minutes, all hell is going to break loose on your heads." It was a complete bluff. We had nothing to back up our words, and no resources to carry out our warning. But shortly after, all the journalists, including the American, were released and they walked out of the parliament gates unharmed.

On July 4, Bainimarama appointed a respectable merchant banker, Laisenia Qarase, as prime minister. Qarase proceeded to form an interim government with Ratu Josefa Iloilo as the president. All during this time, I maintained close contact with Bainimarama. Finally, on July 13, fifty-six days after being taken, all the hostages, including Prime Minister Chaudhry and President Mara's daughter, were released unharmed. On July 27, George Speight was arrested along with 369 of his followers and charged with treason. Prior to his sentencing, Speight was held on the island of Nukulau, where the gala picnic for Buzz Aldrin had been held. Today, he is serving a life sentence.

In analyzing the reasons for the coup, it seems as if the land issue may have been the final catalyst. Indigenous Fijians owned more than eighty percent of the land and regarded it as their sacred birthright. Chaudhry had made changes aimed at stopping indigenous landowners from evicting ethnic Indian tenants, giving those tenants $14,000 (Fijian) in compensation if they lost their leases. Many indigenous landowners saw this as a first step toward an Indian takeover of their land and used it to draw a line in the sand. They considered it as an egregious violation of their birth right. George Speight climbed aboard and rode this sentiment all the way to a coup.

In late July, my government recalled me to Washington D.C. for consultation. I was happy to be reunited with my family. We all returned to Fiji in early August amidst heightened political uncertainty and insecurity. The disruption in schooling for the children was a big issue for us. Omar, who was a senior, was accepted by Monash University in Melbourne, Australia, as a special student where he could finish his high school's prescribed International Baccalaureate program and subsequently be eligible to enroll in the university's undergraduate program. Omar left for Australia at the age of seventeen under these difficult circumstances and we were all saddened to see him go. The other kids remained at ISS despite grave concerns for their security. Life was not the same for us in Suva again.

Upon my return, my first order of business was to meet with the new interim prime minister, Laisenia Qarase. As I entered his office he rose to greet me and as we shook hands, I said, "Today, I'm afraid I did not come to discuss rugby with you."

Our conversation turned very serious and I told him we needed to focus on what I called the other three "R's": restoration of constitutional democracy, reconciliation of the issues of the people of Fiji, and reconstruction of the nation's battered economy. The meeting lasted an hour during which I cautioned the new PM that the U.S. would deal with his government "as necessary." I urged him to be more forthright and transparent in his and his government's efforts toward the timely restoration of the democratic government mandated by the Fijian people. I encouraged him to bring out the best in Fijians, who are renowned for their warmth, tolerance, and understanding. Finally, before leaving, I made sure he understood what the term "interim" meant.

On August 1, 2000, I invited General Rabuka back to the residence for a breakfast meeting. He was always frank with me and loved to share his many colorful stories. For my part, I wanted to feel him out on rumblings I had heard from the Great Council of Chiefs and for a general assessment of the overall crisis situation. As we were about to conclude the meeting, Rabuka sprang a surprise on me. "Ambassador," he said. "I'm interested in seeking the appointment of Fiji's next ambassador to the U.S."

Obviously, he wanted me to run the idea past D.C. for a reaction. I told him that it was the prerogative of the Fijian government as to whom they wanted as their next envoy in D.C., and in the absence of any vetting or clearance process, I presumed his nomination could be on a fast-track. But as far as his agrément from my government was concerned, I could not hazard a guess. "Your...extra-constitutional activities could, I imagine, be a matter of intense debate," I said. Then I added, "But at least you can be assured that we would not withhold our agrément based on personal background." Of course, my personal background, in particular my ethnicity, had been an issue for Rabuka when we were seeking his government's agrément. Or had he forgotten? I smiled politely, looked him in the eye, and shook his hand to say goodbye. As I did so, I was struck by the feeling that my words, even carefully chosen, had, along with my body language, given it all away. Rabuka hadn't forgotten at all and he knew exactly what I was saying, even as he smiled and shook my hand in return. The following month, the Fijian government floated the idea of Rabuka's potential United States ambassadorship to the media and introduced it into the diplomatic chatter of both D.C. and Suva. The agrément never reached my desk to be forwarded to the U.S. government. The trial balloon didn't get far, never quite passing the smell test at Foggy Bottom.

Meanwhile, the Fijian crisis continued. Speaking at the annual meeting of the Fiji Chamber of Commerce and Industry on March 24, 2001, I made it clear that Fiji must make an extraordinary commitment to stability and good governance if it wanted to join the global economy. "Fiji, known in the American mindset as a part of the romantic tropical paradise, has now become famous for changing governments often without notice," I said. "For those from the outside world who want to do business in Fiji, this pattern of political change is quite unsettling. Whether it is a sudden change of government, the threat of violence, or a change in investment and tax rules, when instability enters a marketplace, investors flee as businesses fail and the people suffer."

Although the Australian and the New Zealand governments had bigger economic and political footprints in Fiji, I was amazed by the encouragement and support I received from many significant and influential quarters imploring me and my government to play an important role in the resolution of the crisis. This plea came from the political leadership, the military, civil society, and the media.

I also went out of my way to continue my cordial relationships with the tribal chiefs and with members of the Great Council of Chiefs, something that was never a high priority with my predecessors. I felt it was important to meet with them and my visits were received warmly. I was always welcomed by their traditional Kava ceremonies, complete with drums and dances and their colorful straw outfits. It always brought big smiles when I came carrying their favorite gift: Johnny Walker Black Label Whiskey! One high chief told me, "The Aussies and the Kiwis are economic colonialists here. They have their own personal interests and agenda. The United States can be an honest and neutral broker in the resolution of this crisis."

I was determined that America's support for democracy and human rights be signaled at every opportunity. My officers and I took personal risks to get this message out. To me, these principles were, and are, the bedrock of good governance, and not a foreign flower as may be argued by some. Restoration of democratic governance became my raison d'etre. I was convinced by personal experience that political stability was a prerequisite for economic growth. Before the violent overthrow of Fiji's government, we had succeeded in attracting significant investment in the tourism and power sectors. Despite Fiji's modest market, more could be done, but investors would not return until confidence in the rule of law and the country's democratic governance were restored.

I had an additional concern with the unsettled nature of the Fiji government. Almost all of the nations of the South Pacific are small and distant from the U.S. But they are not so inconsequential or remote for another Pacific power: The People's Republic of China. In my time as ambassador, I saw a steady and strong growth of influence from the Chinese. Chinese newcomers were acquiring farms and shops from the Indians leaving the country. They came not just for the pristine beaches. Important sea lanes ran through the islands.

In an interview with *Time* magazine (June 4, 2001), I expressed my concern at our apparent insouciance and cautioned that disinterest on our part would be an invitation for others to partner with the Fiji Islands. Relationships could develop that may not be in our long-term strategic interests. "Since the cold war ended, we have relaxed here," I said. "We need to pay a bit more attention in this Pacific arena. We are not going to give up our principles, but at the same time we have to figure out ways that we don't let (the Chinese) have a free run of the place."

I also expressed my position to certain high-level policymakers in Washington. I suggested that we engage with strongman Bainimarama and seek his cooperation in sorting out the crisis. I also wondered where the integrity of our government's policies was in this regard. Were we not fully cooperating with a few of the world's foremost and ruthless dictators and rulers? Hosni Mubarak of Egypt came to mind. I understood that Egypt might have had different sets of strategic importance for the U.S., but the principle of the matter could not be argued. Or how about Augusto Pinochet, who took power in Chile following a U.S.-backed coup d'état in 1973? We helped overthrow the democratically elected government of Salvadore Allende. Pinochet became a dictator, executing hundreds of his political rivals and imprisoning tens of thousands, all while the U.S. looked the other way. Let us not make the small island nation of Fiji the poster child of bad behavior when we have cozied up to many such bad actors in the past, I implored. It seemed to me that the double standard of our policy was so transparent on this matter that the entire world noticed it, making our subsequent good intentions lack in credibility.

Although I had the support of PACOM, my petition to engage with Frank Bainimarama and work with him to bring about the necessary changes was strongly contested and ultimately disregarded. In retrospect, I have been proven correct. Close to twenty years later, Prime Minister Frank Bainimarama, now in his second term, is still in full control of Fiji's destiny and the Chinese axis is more influential than ever.

While I was engaged in the restoration of democracy in Fiji, preparations were afoot in my country to hold the 2000 presidential election between Vice President Al Gore, the nominee of the Democratic party, and the governor of Texas, George W Bush, the nominee of the Republican party. On election day, November 3, 2000, the embassy organized a big election day party at a local hotel. I invited cross-sections of Fijians to witness and observe the deliberations of one of the most important events in our democracy—the smooth transition of power, respecting the will of the people exercised by a constitutional right to vote freely. Although it was a tight election marred by voting anomalies in selected precincts in Florida, the message was clear: the rule of law prevails and the people decide who their next leaders will be. The Supreme Court ultimately gave a verdict in favor of George W. Bush as the forty-third president of the United States.

Ambassadors, as per our constitution, are appointed by the president and the commander-in-chief as his or her personal representative. With the election of a new president, all ambassadors, career or political, must submit their resignations effective the day the new president takes oath of office. Customarily, the incoming president asks most career ambassadors to stay on and complete their term. The resignation letters of political ambassadors like me are generally accepted, particularly if the president-elect comes from the opposing party. But because of the unsettled nature of the politics in Fiji, I was asked by President George W. Bush to stay on as long as was necessary to complete the sensitive and important work I was doing in its political transition. Of course, I accepted. The extra time also helped accommodate my children's end of school term, which already had been severely disrupted.

I was proud and honored to serve under two United States presidents. Ultimately, during the summer of 2001, I ended my term as U.S. ambassador. Catherine and the kids and I started for home. But first, we made a stop in Melbourne, Australia for, at long last, some *un*official business. We needed some personal time as a family. Our major priority: some much-needed rest and relaxation. I felt we'd earned it.

CHAPTER FIFTEEN

From the Outside Looking In

We arrived in Melbourne, Australia for our R&R and were delighted to meet up with Omar. We rented a historic brick house in East Melbourne surrounded by Fitzroy Gardens and the Yarra river. It was an idyllic little place and we all looked forward to a great time ahead. All my adult life, I'd had a very rigorous and regimented schedule. For the first time, I felt unburdened and relaxed. And our vacation turned out to be everything we'd hoped for and more. We snorkeled in the Great Barrier Reef, star gazed in the open skies of the Outback, climbed the magical Uluru mountain, enjoyed the beautiful sandy beaches of Brisbane, and observed with wonder the kangaroos, koalas, and wombats in Tasmania. We discovered newfound vistas in New Zealand and enjoyed deliciously French-infused cuisine in Vanuatu. Life was good.

So good, in fact, that we decided to extend our brief sojourn. Catherine and I became enamored by Melbourne, its warm and friendly people and the healthy outdoors. Living down under was too inviting to resist. We admitted our other three children into the local school and we settled in.

In a few months, however, Washington was calling. But in a different sort of way this time. I was invited to join several multinational company boards and was offered advisory positions by a few of them. The Gulf War had created opportunities for several defense contractors. They needed help to navigate the dangerous region and avoid possible pitfalls and hazards. I rented an apartment in Northern Virginia, shuttling between D.C. and Melbourne and raking in significant frequent flier miles. This I did for a few years and then eventually, we all moved back to the States and settled into our old neighborhood of McLean. We had loved our time abroad, but of course we were happy to be back home.

American politics was still infused in my blood, and the excitement of a presidential campaign was like adrenaline flowing through it. There was the 2004 presidential campaign of Senator John Kerry, in which I participated heavily per the encouragement of Ted Kennedy, and the 2008 campaign of Hillary Clinton where my support was eventually merged into Barack Obama's campaign. Of course, I supported President Obama in 2012, as well.

And then, in 2016, Hillary won the Democratic nomination for the presidency and once again I was all in. As the campaign got underway, I was invited to join Hillary's foreign policy team, specifically the Middle East Working Group. I was also a member of the finance team and worked closely with Harold

Ickes, the chairman of Priorities USA, a super PAC aligned with the Democratic platform.

Of course we all thought the campaign would be successful and the results were nothing less than stunning, defying all the polls and pundits. Later, the intelligence community confirmed Russian interference in the electoral process. It remains a matter of conjecture as to whether Hillary would have won absent this intrusion, but it must be said that the very thought of foreign meddling is unacceptable and grossly reprehensible. Whatever may be the political beliefs of any American, certainly we can all agree that an external force or power can never be allowed to influence and convolute our sacred voting process. Our democratic institutions cannot be contaminated by any vested quarters, and we must never, ever allow this to happen in our country. Eternal vigilance is the price of liberty.

Politically, today, I find myself physically on the outside looking in, witnessing with occasional bewilderment the actions of the current administration. Yet, through various political organizations, I'm still very much involved and no less interested in our democratic processes. This is a time when we should all be interested and alert, and participate where we can, no matter where on the political spectrum we find ourselves.

The United States has transformed radically in the past few years, both in opinion and action. Conflict has taken hold in seemingly everything, from ethnicity to religion, gender, and political party. In a sense, many Americans have become radicalized. Whereas the Nazis, Soviets, and the Chinese used basic propaganda, mostly via newspaper, public meetings, and television or films to radicalize their citizens, today's bullhorn is social media—Twitter, Facebook, Instagram and other forums where hateful messages are disseminated to millions of Americans in nanoseconds.

Evidence of this mounting problem is clear. While crime is generally falling in America, hate crimes continue to rise every year. Since 2014, according to FBI data, hate crimes motivated by religion have spiked by fifty-three percent. During the same period, the number of racially motivated incidents increased by twenty-five percent. It's worth asking whether these numbers are anomalies, or rather that we're witnessing the leading edge of a new, perilous time in American history. The relative peace and order of our society since the Second World War seems at risk. Yes, we have had moments of upheaval (the turmoil of the 1960s comes to mind), but something about today's climate feels different somehow— more serious, more dangerous, more ominous.

This unsettling climate is not confined to the U.S., of course. Indeed, perhaps we are only reflecting a more global vulnerability to peace and order. Much has been accomplished by the free peoples of the world. More people are availing themselves of the genius of free markets, upholding human rights, and celebrating our common humanity. But this progress is not spread evenly across the planet. The disparity in earnings and wealth inequality between the rich and the poor is widening. Good healthcare and quality education are reserved for only the few who can afford it. Corruption, especially in third-world and developing economies, is widespread and systemic. Everywhere, the middle class is squeezed and suffering in broad daylight. "Injustice anywhere," Martin Luther King, Jr. admonished, "is a threat to justice everywhere."

All of this provides the ingredients for radicalization on a global level. Author and theologian Karen Armstrong has argued that these developments have ignited the sparks of fundamentalism within organized religion. We have seen violence perpetrated by religious zealots who, in their warped minds, are determined not to accept the positive change of the world, unable to move forward with time and progress. To further their cause, they are willing to kill themselves and others in the name of their faith, which they believe represents the one and only truth. In her illuminating book *The Battle for God: A History of Fundamentalism*, Armstrong says, "There have always been people, in every age and in each tradition, who have fought the modernity of their day." But what we're seeing now is different, as Armstrong argues: "The fundamental movements that have evolved in our own day have a symbiotic relationship with modernity. They may reject the scientific rationalism of the West, but they cannot escape it. Western civilization has changed the world. Nothing—including religion—can ever be the same again." Today's brand of radicalization/ fundamentalism is the byproduct of the progress we have seen in the last decades.

Nowhere has this irrational and demented fundamentalism struck with more disastrous consequences than in the Muslim world where prejudices often overtake reason. As a Muslim, let me be very loud and clear in saying that Islamic fundamentalists who succumb to radicalization and become transformed into terrorists are *not* the voice of Islam. They represent a tiny minority and, not unlike terrorist groups who align themselves with other theologies, are loathed by the mainstream followers. There are many faces to Islam, the vast majority of which espouse a religion of peace, full of mercy and love. This is the Islam I know, the Islam that I grew up with. It is, first and foremost, a religion of compassion. Although the actions of a few misguided individuals in our times may have obscured the compassion that flows forth from the very nature of the Islamic way, it remains an incontrovertible fact that mercy, generosity, and kindness predominate over our primitive instincts. This is the divine nature of Islam. The people who are endangering us are far removed from it.

Crafting a meaningful response to radicalization requires that both the symptoms and the causes be examined and understood. What's needed above all else is a courageous and dispassionate self-examination and introspection. What's ultimately required is a willingness, if necessary, to modify policy. There are essentially two dimensions to an examination of causes. First, we need to reevaluate the way we manage global issues. The world does not fully comprehend what drives the disparate tumult in the streets of Brussels, London, Washington D.C., Paris, Hong Kong, Tokyo, Frankfurt or a host of other cities. Policymakers gather in these cities and elsewhere to negotiate greater economic liberalization according to agendas inspired by powerful governments (and not only the U.S.) and by freewheeling enterprises. But the impacts of modern globalization are *not* closing the gaps between the haves and have-nots within and between countries. For many, individual security and cultural integrity are under attack. A more equitable order that does not privilege one set of interests over all others is clearly needed. A revitalized and adequately resourced international system qualified to handle the challenges of the inequities of the twenty-first century is required. In order to prevail in the long run over the wide disparities that have become the symptoms of our age, along with the attenuating terrorism and its

affiliated scourges like drugs, money-laundering, human traf-
ficking, cyber-threats, etcetera, a genuine collective return to
global cooperation is the only way.

Secondly, we need to revisit our Middle East policy. It is
unrealistic to believe we can win our war on terror with the
status quo of the region. The conflicts in places like Syria, Libya,
Bahrain, Yemen, Iraq, Algeria, and Tunisia, are wildfires that
risk breaking containment, threatening to burn us all. We must
have a viable, long-term strategy to deal appropriately with these
flashpoints. Furthermore, there can no longer be any argument
about the permanence of the State of Israel. And there can no
longer be a zero-sum approach to the conflict. What is good for
Israel is not necessarily bad for the Palestinians, and vice-versa.
And what is good for both the Israelis and the Palestinians is a
mutually acceptable, two-state resolution of their heart-rending
conflict. Accommodation of the Palestinian aspirations might
be politically hard, and perhaps be immeasurably painful, but
the alternative of not doing anything could be much, much
worse.

The presence of Muslims around the world and in the United
States presents a similar dynamic for most people. There are 1.8
billion Muslims in the world today, forming a majority in fifty-seven countries across North Africa, the Middle East, Asia
Minor, and Central/South/Southeast Asia. While Islam is currently the world's second-largest religion (after Christianity), it
is also the fastest-growing among the major religions. Tellingly,
the Middle East/North Africa regions, where the religion orig-
inated in the seventh century, is home to only about twenty
percent of the world's Muslims. Eighty percent live elsewhere
around the globe.

In the U.S., the profile of the American Muslim is hard to pin down. For certain, it is not the stereotypical image of the Arab. The roots of Islam in the U.S. go back to the days of slavery where it trickled into the Native American tribes. Today, approximately three and a half million Americans (about 1.1 percent of the nation's population) are Muslims, based on a 2017 census study. The census's demographic projections estimate that Muslims will make up 2.1 percent of the population by the year 2050, surpassing the Jewish population as the second-largest faith group in the country.

A Pew study conducted in 2017 asked Americans to rate members of nine religious groups on a "feeling thermometer," ranging from zero to one-hundred degrees. Overall, Americans gave Muslims an average rating of forty-eight degrees, behind Jews, Catholics, Protestants, Buddhists, Hindus, and Mormons. Republicans and those who lean toward the Republican Party gave Muslims an average rating of thirty-nine, significantly cooler than the Democrats' rating of fifty-six. Republicans are also more likely than Democrats to say that Islam is not part of mainstream American society (sixty-eight percent versus thirty-seven percent) and that there is a natural conflict between Islam and democracy (sixty-five percent versus thirty percent). About half of Americans (forty-nine percent) think at least "some" U.S. Muslims are anti-American, greater than the share who say "just a few" or "none."

Views on this question have become a lot more partisan since September 11, 2001. Mistrust has dominated relations between Muslims and Christians for the past two decades. Two overriding reasons could be the worsening of some political problems that have religious components to them (e.g., the

Palestinian issue, the War on Terror), and negative public opinion of Islam, exacerbated at times with violence by certain Muslim factions.

The message of religion can be used as a major force of unification among divergent factions and therefore can play a key role in the promotion of global peace and reconciliation. Religion has its power, but the misuse of religion can be even more powerful. Interfaith dialogue therefore must play a critical role in the field of social and cultural diplomacy.

It is not human nature for one to abdicate his or her own identity and culture, however overwhelming may be one's empathy and admiration for the other. But recognizing differences and accepting the legitimacy of the others is an honorable and righteous accomplishment that enhances our common humanity, our faith and tolerance of others. We need to accelerate the process of discovering a new way for religions and cultures to be in dialogue, which will be of service in fostering peace, security, and stability in the world. Engagement, dialogue, discussion—all of these presume that we will not always agree. But the alternative, a refusal to engage and dialogue and discuss, is most certainly a recipe for far worse than mere disagreement.

We are a pluralistic society. It is what gives us our strength. But, of course, this plurality extends beyond religion. Today, we are mired in critical debates about immigration. "Give me your tired, your poor, your huddled masses yearning to breathe free, the wretched refuse of your teeming shore," reads the inscription, written by Emma Lazarus in 1883, at the base of the Statue of Liberty. To this day, I find myself feeling emotional whenever I think back to that first time I gazed out at Lady Liberty. She's been welcoming immigrants to our shores since 1886. How relevant is her inscription today?

According to the U.S. Census Bureau, immigrants comprise about fourteen percent of our population. Together, immigrants and their U.S. born children make up twenty-seven percent of the total U.S. population. The undocumented population is about eleven million and has stayed pretty much at that number since the economic crisis in 2008. Though many policies that aim to reduce unlawful immigration focus on border security, most undocumented immigrants are overstays, having arrived in the U.S. legally. The United States granted 1.1 million permanent residencies in 2017.

As for the workforce, immigrants make up roughly seventeen percent of it, according to a Pew study. Immigrants make up forty-five percent of domestic employees, thirty-six percent of textile workers, thirty-three percent of agriculture workers, and thirty-two percent of those employed in the hospitality business. Imagine the United States economy without these workers. The U.S. has benefitted, and will continue to benefit, immensely from immigration.

The conundrum we are faced with is how to balance and streamline our immigration policy to allow a sensible and acceptable flow of legal immigrants without creating structural or social imbalances in our workforce. I am opposed to illegal immigration and all disincentives should be in place to deter it. But I also believe that our country was built on the backs of immigrants and future progress depends upon it.

I am not alone. A 2019 Gallup poll found seventy-six percent of Americans consider immigration a good thing. As many as eighty-one percent support a path to citizenship for undocumented immigrants if they meet certain criteria. A 2016 Gallup survey found that seventy-six percent of Republicans support citizenship more than a proposed border wall.

Some say that the U.S. does not have an immigration problem; it has a refugee problem. This is worth examining. Why *do* people leave their homes, their families, any or all of their possessions, for some faraway land with no certainty? There are three kinds of refugees: economic, political/humanitarian, and a new category that I call climate refugees. Economic refugees (from Mexico, Honduras, El Salvador, etc.) are looking for better standards of living. Political refugees (from Syria, Venezuela, Iran, Myanmar, etc.) leave their countries out of fear of persecution and to avoid conditions such as law and order breakdowns, extrajudicial killings, and gang warfare. The third refugee is a new phenomenon, but one I predict we'll be hearing more and more about. Consider the small island nation of Tuvalu, which I got to know well in my time as ambassador. Small rises in average temperatures can potentially have a devastating effect on such a place. With the current pace of rising sea levels, Tuvalu might be uninhabitable in just a few decades. In the interim, because of climate change, we are seeing an increase in weather-related disasters like hurricanes and floods and droughts, thus leading to displacement, especially from poorer countries that do not have the wherewithal to rebuild.

All of the refugee crises that we see, no matter the reason, are significant, but none are more urgent and more dangerous than the conditions that lead to a wide-scale political refugee crisis. We have seen catastrophic displacement of citizens in places like Syria, Iraq, and Venezuela. Recently, we have seen the systematic genocide of the Rohingya minority in Myanmar.

Led by Nobel Peace Laureate and de facto head of state, Aung San Suu Kyi, the Rohingya people have been subjected to extreme violence. Greater than a million have been pushed into neighboring Bangladesh. Despite international assistance, this sudden influx of refugees has put Bangladesh in an untenable situation. The country, with a population of about 167 million, has a land mass of about 58,000 square miles, smaller in area than the state of Wisconsin, which has a population of just 5.8 million. Wisconsin's population would have to increase by close to thirty times before it would have the density of the nation of Bangladesh. Looked at another way, the current density of Bangladesh is 2,931 people per square mile. If you took the totality of the world's current population (including China's 1.4 billion and India's 1.3 billion) and put it all in the United States, the density would only be 1,974 per square mile, roughly a third less dense than today's Bangladesh. And yet Rohingya refugees continue to add to Bangladesh's burgeoning population. In accepting these people, the citizens of Bangladesh, *despite their own poverty*, have acted on moral and humanitarian grounds.

For all the controversy and debate, do we have an immigration problem in the United States? Do we not have room in this country for immigrants who are escaping economic hardships, political persecution, or crises caused by climate change? Yes, we need an immigration policy that provides strong deterrence for illegal entry through our land borders, airports, and seaports, a policy that bolsters security and lessens the economic threat to our existing labor pools. But we also need a policy based on humanitarianism, and one that understands what was at the very root of this country's growth and progress. We need an immigration policy that reduces long and unproductive backlogs for legal applicants and encourages the movement into this great nation of the kind of people that we can be proud to call "Americans."

One vital component for the success of our country moving forward is the education of its youth. To prepare young people to face their future effectively in our rapidly changing world is a moral responsibility of this nation's leaders. America is considered a powerhouse worldwide because of its prestigious schools and colleges. A degree from a renowned American college or university is like a Super Bowl trophy, and young adults from all over the world aspire to avail themselves of this opportunity. According to estimates, young adults in America earn fifty-seven percent more if they have a bachelor's degree than if they only complete high school.

Today, we are embroiled in a fierce debate on the question of whether college education should be free for all in America. One can easily see the importance of the question. Outstanding student loans are now estimated at $1.5 *trillion*. Emotions run high on both sides of the debate, but the answer is not a simple yes or no. The issue deserves an open-minded, dispassionate, and balanced understanding of the potential benefits, drawbacks, and alternatives.

Proponents of free college believe that it would benefit not only the recipient but the nation as a whole. Those making the case for free education argue that it is not just an economic one, but also one with moral and philosophical implications. Opponents of free college tend to believe that the idea is expensive (leading to much higher taxation), unnecessary, and not sustainable in the long run. Realistically speaking, is free college free? Someone must pay for it, of course. Raising taxes on the wealthiest, closing corporate loopholes, implementing new taxes on Wall Street transactions, decreasing military expenditures, and cracking down on government waste could be a few pathways to finance such an undertaking, none of which would come without heavy resistance.

While this debate is going on, roughly 32 million adults in our country, or fourteen percent of the population, are functionally illiterate, according to the U.S. Department of Education and the National Institute of Literacy. Perhaps there exist middle-ground solutions. Australia has a very successful program called Higher Education Loan Program (HELP), an income-based, interest-free, student aid program based on an affordable economic matrix. Other ideas could be to expand the existing Pell Grant program, incentives for colleges/universities to lower their costs, and/or discouraging the distribution of merit-based financial aid to wealthy students. These are the solutions I feel are most worthy of exploration. But we cannot afford to procrastinate. Education will be one of the most important factors in determining the future progress of our nation. We have to get it right.

Health care is another especially contentious issue that presents challenges, with some advocating for it in a free and universal way. Already, entitlement programs take up close to sixty percent of the federal budget. As this book is going to press, the current budget deficit for the year is projected to be $1.1 trillion with our nation's total debt at *$23 trillion*. (I can't help but feel compelled to note here that during his term, my boss, President Clinton balanced the budget and when he left office in 2000, he left the budget with a surplus.) The interest payment to service today's debt is approximately $400 billion per year. I am in favor of access to quality healthcare by all Americans. Yet, we cannot bankrupt our country to make it so. Alternatives must be found and the solution must include freedom of choice. Social security is an entitlement, and yet we are free to decline it if we so choose, and we are further free to arrange our own retirement plans. We would never allow the government to tell us how to invest for our retirement or limit us to a single retirement vehicle. I'm all in favor of a safety net, but why should we consider allowing the government to tell us what to do with our healthcare, limiting us in our choices? Whatever the ultimate solution, like education, healthcare is not an issue that can afford to wait.

I can't close these rambling, political thoughts of mine without quickly addressing the climate change issue mentioned above. From an idea to a theory to a prediction to a reality and now to an emergency, climate change is a global phenomenon that does not respect any borders. It is impacting every country on the planet, disrupting national economies, affecting lives, and costing society dearly. Weather patterns are changing, sea levels are rising, and greenhouse gas emissions are at their highest. Hurricanes, flooding, and tsunamis are getting ferociously stronger with increasing frequency. Without action, the average world temperature is expected to rise over three degrees centigrade by the turn of the next century. The poorest and the weakest are most vulnerable and will bear this disaster more than others. There is no time to hesitate on this issue and no time to fence-sit. The stakes are too high. We must all be involved. "The hottest places in hell," John F. Kennedy said, "are reserved for those who, in times of great moral crisis, maintain their neutrality."

I am hopeful, by the pace of change that many countries are adopting, that we'll be able to combat this danger. Results thus far have been slightly encouraging, although the jury is still out. Increasing numbers of countries are reverting to renewable energy, whether it be solar or wind, and taking effective measures to reduce their carbon footprint. The automobile and trucking industries are leapfrogging their efforts toward converting from fossil fuel to electric power.

The Paris climate accord of 2016 was a big step in the right direction. In that agreement, all signatory countries agreed to limit the rise of global temperature to less than two degrees centigrade. By 2018, 175 parties ratified the agreement. Unfortunately, the Trump administration decided to unilaterally pull out of it. The failure of governments to act in the face of the insurmountable scientific evidence for climate change would be the biggest human rights violation of this century. I'll remain hopeful that wisdom will prevail and my generation will leave to future generations an intact, unharmed earth, full of the promise that belonged to humankind at the very dawn of our civilization. It is our duty. It is our responsibility, not just as Americans, but as human beings.

EPILOGUE

IN MY LIFE, I'VE HAD many uniquely "American" experiences. Two stand out for their remarkable significance. The first was my achievement in the business world. What I was able to accomplish from the ground up, with minimal capital and wherewithal, and the odds stacked against me, is a testament to American capitalism and free enterprise. The second was my appointment by President Clinton to represent the United States of America as an ambassador. How beautifully American that a first-generation immigrant of South-Asian/Muslim descent could be granted the opportunity of such a high office and be allowed to stand shoulder to shoulder on the world stage with leaders and dignitaries and people of great influence.

America is the land of opportunity. We hear this so much that I fear it's become a cliché, falling these days on deaf ears. But sometimes, there is a reason that an assertion becomes a cliché and the reason is that the assertion is an undeniable truth. Lest you have any doubts, I submit my story as evidence of that truth. This is my testimony. The world is a beautiful, fascinating place full of extraordinary people and awe-inspiring wonders, and I have seen much of it. But whenever I travel abroad, I eventually find myself yearning to return home. And that home is the United States of America, the land that has given me so much. The land that gave me, above all else, opportunity.

My one lament is that I cannot make certain people see this country through my eyes. Based on today's political dialogue, you'd think this nation is failing in every conceivable way. So many people are anguished. Americans go at each other in ways that would have been foreign to generations past. The national conversation is prickly and blunt and almost always divisive. Lost in the haze of it all is that beautiful and prosperous country that I know, where anyone can aspire to be someone of their own choosing. Why has our peaceful, law-abiding society turned into a pitched battleground of mistrust? Why are we seeing so much anti-Semitism, xenophobia, and hatred? Why are we witnessing mass shootings in schools, churches, synagogues, mosques, and malls? Why has healthy debate been replaced by vicious, visceral, vitriolic diatribes? Why are vengeful fantasies and unspeakable anger being unleashed online? What has happened to our institutional safeguards and guardrails?

Why, as well, are there people who continue to accuse the press of being the enemy of the state? I believe that an independent and vibrant press is the collective conscience of a nation. Any efforts to subdue or subjugate it to the whims of the personality or group is an outright affront to democracy.

The founding commitments of America were to democracy, human rights, and the rule of law. Many have labeled them as the soul, spirit, and genius of our nation. And over the generations, our citizens have given their lives to preserve these commitments. At times, it now appears that their true meanings have eroded. Long-settled truths have opened to new interpretations and spins. Is this a symptom or a cause of what some see as our current crisis? Does America face erosion of public faith in our political institutions?

Are we a nation in decline?

I still believe in America, the home of Lincoln and King, Jefferson and Kennedy, Roosevelt and Reagan, a nation whose Founding Fathers enshrined in its charter the right to question authority, the right to liberty, the right to free speech, the right to practice individual religion, the right to exercise our franchise without fear or favor. All of these and more as we pursue our right to be happy.

In my humble judgment, as we move forward, our capacity to correct course, our ability to discern between right and wrong, and, most importantly, our collective faith in the goodness of our own people will enable America to regain its rightful place of leadership in the community of nations. We are a family. We love each other; at times we hate each other. We fight, we make peace. To the cynics and pessimists, I offer my earlier analogy. We are Bus USA, hitting the inevitable potholes, bouncing around in our seats, but hanging on, knowing the suspension is reliable, a suspension built on the flexibility of the U.S. Constitution. Change is allowed for; change is welcome. In the long run, I am convinced that cooler heads will prevail. Those who eschew the hyperbole and shrillness of today's political discourse in favor of a reasonable, rational, thinking, and encompassing approach toward today's problems will ultimately win the day. Solutions will be found in careful contemplation, with the goal of bringing the country together, not further dividing it.

Stepping back and looking at our state of affairs not as political beings but as human beings, our divisions present themselves as largely contrived. As spoken by President Dwight D. Eisenhower at the Centennial Commencement Address of Pennsylvania State University, June 11, 1955, "If we are to have partners for peace, then we must first be partners in sympathetic recognition that all mankind possesses in common like aspirations and hungers, like ideals and appetites, like purposes and frailties, a like demand for economic development. The divisions between us are artificial and transient. Our common humanity is God-made and enduring."

By the middle of this century, some thirty years from now, when the calendar will mark the year 2050 and, by chance, I might still be alive at 100 years of age, what kind of civilization might we be living in? Will climate change have engulfed some significant portion of the land masses that make up today's geography? Will the world population, at close to ten billion, according to United Nations projections, look at settlements beyond our known planet? Will we totally eradicate scourges like cancer, diabetes, Alzheimer's, and other diseases? Will artificial intelligence overtake human rationality? How will we have handled the vicissitudes of life on planet Earth?

I don't think I have a good answer to any of these questions. However, I'm confident that human ingenuity will survive and goodwill shall prevail over evil, mutually assisted destruction of nuclear stockpiles will happen, diseases will be conquered, and rainforests and glaciers will be saved. Humankind will be fine and America will be fine. Our nation will continue to provide a light to the world. We will continue to be a beacon of hope. We will continue to be a land of opportunity. I believe in all of this as surely as I believe that each morning the sun will shine first on the shores of Fiji. These are leaps of faith I will always be willing to take.

ACKNOWLEDGEMENTS

THE IDEA OF WRITING MY memoir had been on my mind for quite some time, but when I tried to muster my efforts toward its realization, I quickly discovered that the job was a lot bigger than what I had originally anticipated. Fortunately, I had the support, blessings, and cooperation of the people mentioned below. Without them, the task would have remained unfulfilled.

First, I'd like to thank President Bill Clinton and Hillary Clinton for their enthusiastic support of this book. My discussions with them reinforced my resolve to go through this arduous process, for which I am very grateful. I have always valued their judgement and input. Additionally, I can't underscore enough the support I received from those close to them, especially Huma Abedin for her encouragement and Oscar Flores for his invaluable guidance and support.

The critical advice on the framing of events that I received from Ambassador J. Douglas Holladay, himself a prolific writer, was considerable. Ambassador Ronald K. McMullen's verification and clarification of facts and events while serving with me at Embassy Suva were immensely helpful.

Much appreciation to Governor Terry McAuliffe, an old friend and a fellow party loyalist from whom I learned much about politics on a national level; Admiral (retd.) Dennis C. Blair, a trusted advisor and friend; and Peter Bergen, an admired author and political commentator, whose books I have always enjoyed including his latest, *Trump and His Generals.* Their reviews of the manuscript and kind comments strengthened my resolve to get this book, finally, to print.

I'm grateful for David Rubenstein's thoughtful comments. David inspires many like me not only because of his extraordinary business successes but also because of his enduring outreach for the preservation of our art, culture, and history. His philanthropy has made America richer.

My wife, Catherine, has always been a source of inspiration to me. Her questioning and correction of the manuscript transformed this testimony into a credible product. She has been meticulous on the validation and verification of facts and has kept me honest, making me a better author, just as she has always made me a better person.

My children have been a source of inspiration, as well, showing their enthusiasm, motivating me to persevere, and insistently connecting important dots in the story that I would otherwise have missed. This book is better because of their participation.

I've had tremendous support from all my close and extended family members and they are just too many to mention. However, I'd be remiss if I didn't acknowledge the interest and support I received from my sister-in-law Veronique who was relentless in keeping me focused on the book.

Also, my nephew Ron Wahid and his wife Magdalena inspired me to write with an eye toward reaching beyond myself to arrive at a book of higher political and social ideals. For that, writing this book has become much more worthwhile. I am truly blessed.

Finally, it would have not been possible to undertake this project without the close cooperation and active collaboration of my editor Jerry Payne. He was with me every step of the way, from helping me hammer out the structure to helping me finalize the manuscript. He kept me on point, he kept me moving forward, and he kept it fun. Most of all, he made it happen. What more could I have asked?

INDEX

ABOUT THE AUTHOR

M. OSMAN SIDDIQUE IS AMERICA'S first serving Muslim ambassador and chief of mission. Born in East Pakistan, Ambassador Siddique was witness to the violent birth of a new country as East Pakistan became Bangladesh. Seeking the promise and opportunity of the United States, he left Bangladesh to complete his academic studies at Indiana University in Bloomington, in the heartland of America. After a stint with a Fortune 500 company, he became a prolific entrepreneur and, most proudly, an American citizen. Political service followed and, in 1999, President Clinton appointed Siddique ambassador to Fiji, Tonga, Tuvalu, and Nauru. Following the 2000 Fijian paramilitary coup, Ambassador Siddique played a critical role in the restoration of democracy and the rehabilitation of that country.

With his wife, Catherine, Siddique lives in McLean, Virginia where he remains intricately involved in the political, economic, and social discourse of our nation.